ISO 9000:2000 In a Nutshell

A Concise Guide to the Revisions

Second Edition

Jeanne Ketola
&
Kathy Roberts

Paton Press

Chico, California

Most Paton Press books are available at quantity discounts when purchased in bulk. For more information, contact:

Paton Press
P.O. Box 44
Chico, CA 95927-0044
Telephone: (530) 342-5480
Fax: (530) 342-5471
E-mail: *books@patonpress.com*
Web: *www.patonpress.com*

ISBN 0-9650445-9-9

Notice of Rights

Notice of Liability

Staff

Publisher	Scott M. Paton
Senior Editor	Vanessa R. Franco
Assistant Editor	Heidi M. Paton
Book Cover Design	Edward C. Jones

Dedication

To Mom and Dad, who always said I could;
Chuck, Tim, Lida, and Jon, who inspire me every day;
My clients, who challenge themselves to be the best.

—Jeanne

To Ryan, who is my soulmate and best friend,
and to Austin, who is my pride and joy.
Thanks for reminding me what's important in life.

—Kathy

Contents

Dedication .... *v*

1 Introduction 1
2 Process Management 5
3 Comparing ISO 9001:1994 with ISO 9001:2000 15
    4.1 Management Responsibility 16
    4.2 Quality System 23
    4.3 Contract Review 27
    4.4 Design Control 30
    4.5 Document and Data Control 34
    4.6 Purchasing 37
    4.7 Control of Customer-Supplied Product 41
    4.8 Product Identification and Traceability 43
    4.9 Process Control 45
    4.10 Inspection and Testing 48
    4.11 Control of Inspection, Measuring, and Test Equipment 52
    4.12 Inspection and Test Status 56
    4.13 Control of Nonconforming Product 58
    4.14 Corrective and Preventive Action 61
    4.15 Handling, Storage, Packaging, Preservation, and Delivery ... 65
    4.16 Control of Quality Records 68
    4.17 Internal Quality Audits 72
    4.18 Training 75
    4.19 Servicing 78
    4.20 Statistical Techniques 80

4 Noteworthy Changes 83
5 Transition Planning 89
6 Answers to Common Concerns 97

Appendixes
1 Record Requirements 105
2 Clause-to-Section Cross-Reference Matrix 107

About the Authors 111
Index 113

Chapter 1

Introduction

For many organizations, the revisions to the ISO 9000 family of standards will cause panic, shock, and confusion. For others, the transition from the old to the new will seem brief and relatively painless. The ease with which an organization adapts will depend largely on the maturity of its quality management system and the commitment of top management to continual improvement.

Much has been written about the revisions to the ISO 9000 series. As the revisions passed each iteration on their path to becoming a released international standard, the public had the opportunity to review the progress and comment on the drafts by means of a standardized template submitted to the American Society for Quality. Web sites are also available to provide information on the changes. *(See Chapter 6 for a list of information sources on the new standards.)*

The consolidation of the ISO 9000 series consists of the following four core documents, plus *ISO 10012 Measurement Control System* (a combination of *ISO 10012-1:1992 Metrological confirmation system for measuring equipment* and *ISO 10012-2:1997 Guideline for control of measurement processes*):

■ *ISO 9000:2000 Quality management systems—Fundamentals and vocabulary*. This document describes quality management system fundamentals and terminology. It cancels and replaces ISO 8402:1994 and ISO 9000-1:1994, clauses 4 and 5. *ISO 9000-1 Guidelines for the selection and use of the ISO 9000 series* has been published as a brochure by ISO.

■ *ISO 9001:2000 Quality management systems—Requirements*. This document defines the requirements for quality management systems and is used to demonstrate an organization's capability to provide products that meet customer and applicable regulatory requirements. It cancels and replaces ISO 9001:1994, ISO 9002:1994, and ISO 9003:1994. Exclusions, such as design, are allowed for those organizations that have used ISO 9002 and ISO 9003.

■ *ISO 9004:2000 Quality management systems—Guidelines for performance improvement.* This document provides guidance on quality management systems and includes concepts for continual improvement processes that link to customer satisfaction. It is intended to guide top management if they wish to move beyond the requirements of ISO 9001:2000. ISO 9004:2000 and ISO 9001:2000 were developed as a consistent pair. ISO 9004:2000 cancels and replaces ISO 9004-1:1994.

■ *ISO 19011 Guidelines on quality and/or environmental management systems auditing.* This document will provide guidance on managing and conducting quality and environmental audits and is intended to be a joint auditing document. It will cancel and replace ISO 10011.

This book was written with the intent of presenting the revisions to ISO 9001 in a clear and concise manner. The book contains the specific information organizations need to know in order to understand the changes, communicate them to personnel at all levels, and implement the changes with minimal disruption to their systems. This book is unique in that it presents the changes in a format familiar to most organizations: The ISO 9001:2000 revisions are integrated within the 4.1–4.20 structure from the 1994 version. This book will enable organizations to bring their current quality systems to ISO 9001:2000 compliance.

Because ISO 9001:2000 is based on a process management approach, the next chapter of this book focuses on this concept. Chapter 3 compares ISO 9001:2000's "new" requirements to those in the 1994 version. Chapter 4 examines some of the more noteworthy changes to ISO 9001. Chapter 5 offers tips on how to transition from ISO 9001:1994 to ISO 9001:2000. Chapter 6 addresses common concerns that organizations may have and contains a list of resources for more information.

As active members of the U.S. Technical Advisory Group (TAG) to ISO Technical Committee 176 (TC 176), we participated in discussions within Task Group 18. This group was responsible for evaluating the revisions to ISO 9001 and ISO 9004, generating a list of concerns, and developing the U.S. positions on these two standards. The U.S. delegates presented these positions at the international meetings. Because we have been active members for more than six years, we have an in-depth knowledge of the standards-development process and possess first-hand information about the details of the revisions.

In addition to our participation in the U.S. TAG, we own successful management consulting practices specializing in ISO 9000 system implementation. We both have solid backgrounds in management and have worked in a variety of industries. Because we work with all levels of personnel from executive management to line employees, we have an inside view of ISO 9000 implementation. As such, we're able to understand top management's concerns regarding the revisions.

Our intent in writing this book was to provide those responsible for implementing and maintaining ISO 9001:2000 with a simple approach for understanding the revisions, as well as to answer the major questions they may have. We hope that this publication will become a well-used handbook during the change process.

In a nutshell, good luck and happy reading!

Chapter 2

Process Management

One of the first things you'll notice about ISO 9001:2000 is its new structure. The sections are no longer listed as 4.1–4.20, as they were in the 1994 version. ISO 9001:1994 was organized from a functional point of view. As a result, many organizations didn't link their processes together to build a management system. Instead, they organized it by specific areas of responsibility. For example, using ISO 9001:1994 as a basis, engineering would take responsibility for 4.4 Design Control, customer service would take responsibility for 4.3 Contract Review, and the quality function would take responsibility for 4.17 Internal Quality Audits and 4.14 Corrective and Preventive Action. Although the personnel in these functions may do a good job of ensuring that these elements operate within their scope of responsibility, they often don't see how these requirements are linked to or affect other departments or functions.

Many organizations arranged into this functional view, also known as "silos," operate by passing problems on to the next function or department. Often, those in the next function think about the problem, delay, and eventually take action. They may be able to fix what has been sent to them, or they may return the problem to the first department for more information, thus delaying the schedule of activities.

The trouble with the functional view of management is that it fails to assess the business from an entire "systems" perspective necessary for determining the information and activity interfaces between departments. For example, what information does customer service need from sales in order to initiate an order? What information does engineering need to provide to production in order to produce a product? Who needs to be involved in the review of customer requirements? Finally, where does the customer fit into all of this?

In 1997, ISO surveyed a random sample of companies to determine what changes needed to be made to the next revision of the ISO 9000 series. Users complained that the 1994 version was cumbersome, functionally oriented, manufacturing-biased, and nonsystematic, and it failed to link methods for a unified business approach. Users also felt that the year 2000 revision for ISO 9001 should have a process-oriented structure, be customer-focused, and be designed to promote continual improvement.

With this feedback in mind, the ISO Technical Committee 176 Subcommittee 2 developed a process model to depict generic requirements of a quality management system as linked processes *(refer to ISO 9001:2000)*. The model shows that customer input is significant in defining requirements and that it's necessary to evaluate and verify that the requirements are met.

The process model concept is also based on eight quality management principles, which are found in ISO 9000:2000 and ISO 9004:2000 *(refer to Chapter 5, Transition Planning, for a definition of the principles)*:
- Customer focus
- Leadership
- Involvement of people
- Process approach
- System approach to management
- Continual improvement
- Factual approach to decision making
- Mutually beneficial supplier relationships

ISO 9001:2000 attempts to address the basics of a unified approach by breaking down organizational activities into five blocks, which emphasize the process approach in the following order:
- *Quality management system*—Management must establish, document, implement, and maintain a quality management system.
- *Management responsibility*—Management must define and provide evidence of commitment to the development, implementation, and improvement of the quality management system.
- *Resource management*—Management must determine and apply the necessary resources for improvement activities and customer satisfaction.
- *Product realization*—Management must ensure that processes are planned, established, and implemented.

■ *Measurement, analysis and improvement*—Management must implement measurements, analyze them, and use the information from the system as a basis for improvement.

Figure 2.1 shows the five blocks with the corresponding elements from ISO 9001:1994.

Figure 2.1: ISO 9001:1994's clauses in relation to ISO 9001:2000's sections.

Figure 2.2: The systems model of process management.

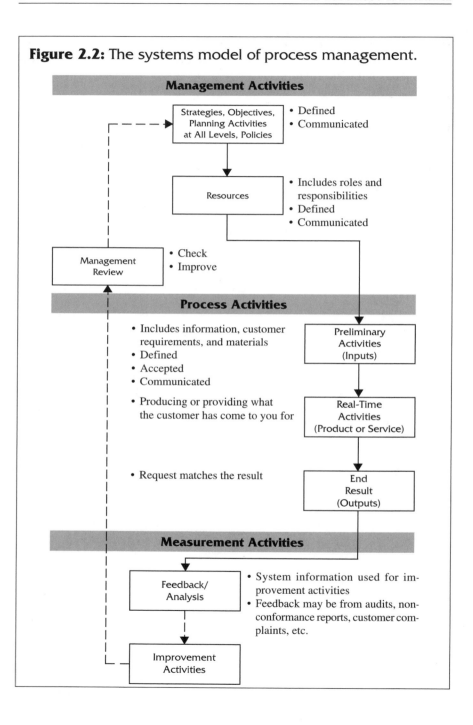

Structuring the organization into these five blocks enables an organization to shift from functional management to process management.

Figure 2.2, the systems model, describes an additional view of process management.

Take the following quiz to determine whether your organization operates from a functional perspective or a process perspective:

1. My organization analyzes existing methods and links between departments and personnel.
a. Always
b. Sometimes
c. Seldom
d. Never

2. Management communicates specific plans for how the quality objectives can be achieved at all levels.
a. Always
b. Sometimes
c. Seldom
d. Never

3. Departments within my organization are willing to work on cross-functional approaches to improve.
a. Always
b. Sometimes
c. Seldom
d. Never

4. Measurement results are communicated, analyzed, and used for improvement activities.
a. Always
b. Sometimes
c. Seldom
d. Never

5. Decisions for improvement activities occur before problems are discovered.
a. Always
b. Sometimes

c. Seldom

d. Never

6. Information is easily exchanged between departments.

a. Always

b. Sometimes

c. Seldom

d. Never

7. My organization clearly understands how each activity within a process affects others, as well as the effect each process has on the entire business.

a. Always

b. Sometimes

c. Seldom

d. Never

8. The personnel in my organization have clearly defined requirements from our customers and understand how to meet their needs and expectations.

a. Always

b. Sometimes

c. Seldom

d. Never

9. Top management takes an active role in reviewing the quality management system, initiating actions for improvements and ensuring that these actions are carried through.

a. Always

b. Sometimes

c. Seldom

d. Never

10. My organization has a formal system for collecting customer satisfaction and dissatisfaction data and uses this information for improvement.

a. Always

b. Sometimes

c. Seldom

d. Never

To score your quiz, count the number of times you selected each letter. Award yourself 5 points for each *a*, 3 points for each *b*, 1 point for each *c*, and 0 points for each *d*. Add your points together for a total.

If you scored 40–50 points, your organization is doing a good-to-excellent job of thinking and managing in process terms. If you scored 35–39 points, your organization may be working toward a process approach but is not doing so consistently. If you scored fewer than 35 points, you are still in a functional mode of management.

PROCESS MANAGEMENT BASICS

The following section covers some of the basic concepts of process management. Let's start with two process definitions:

1. A process is a course, direction, trend, sequence, or method.
2. A process is an end-to-end set of activities that is customer-focused and cross-functional, and it delivers a product and/or service that creates value for the customer.

Both definitions must be considered because all organizations have processes and customers. However, if processes or methods are not clearly defined, end-to-end breakdowns will occur, and ultimately customers will be dissatisfied.

Processes are inherent in all organizations. It would be impossible to produce a product or service without processes. Those organizations that have marginal processes can continue to exist; however, those with *linked* processes are most likely more competitive, innovative, and consistently profitable.

Although organizations that don't have linked processes may be able to address their customers' needs, the degree to which they are able to satisfy their end customers is demonstrated in their ability to consistently execute their processes. For example, suppose that personnel at XYZ Co. tell you that they're far too creative to be locked into disciplines or procedures. What you may discover about XYZ Co. is that its processes or methods are loosely connected, and breakdowns occur frequently between and within departments or functions. Because its methods are not defined, the organization cannot really assess how well it's able to repeat its processes. When product gets out the door, XYZ's personnel consider it a success and don't see the path of destruction or dollars lost in achieving their goal. The path of destruction often shows up in such things as customer complaints, nonconforming product, and employee burnout.

If all organizations have processes, then why change the standard and make such a big deal about process management? Even though organizations have methods in place, the ability to consistently meet their customers' expectations has plagued organizations for years. ISO 9001:2000's mission is to provide a stepping stone from functional management thinking to process management thinking and is structured to facilitate the idea that all processes are linked. Often, organizations look at the nonconforming product or the customer complaint and implement immediate solutions rather than challenging the process. As some organizations recognize, without a connected approach, they operate as if they're playing golf in the dark. Satisfying customers becomes a guessing game: No one knows for certain which hole is being played, what the course looks like, or which club to use. Instead of knowing precisely what comes next, these organizations feel their way along, hoping that the club they're pulling from their bag is the right one.

Organizations that are already registered are not exempt from this dilemma. Some have become registered with weak, disconnected systems. Although they may be working to improve these systems, the emphasis on continually reviewing processes and making the necessary changes may have waned since the certificate arrived.

The necessity for organizations to structure their business as a connected series of events is crucial, and the following four factors need to be considered when moving toward process management.

First, defining and documenting what your organization really does helps you gain an understanding of the methods in place. Unfortunately, documentation gets a bad rap, but until you visually observe the flow of activities, it's next to impossible to reach agreement about and establish a clear picture of the steps. This is a time for honesty and full participation; documentation is not a task that involves only the management representative. Without an analysis of the systems, the methods that were minimally defined in the first place provide little insight when solving problems. When organizations don't take the time to define the details, they can't assess how well they're doing or pinpoint the real cause of problems. The sheer effort of working around systems simply to get products or services out the door on time becomes the mode of operation.

Next, determine how the processes link together and who's responsible for them. It's amazing how many employees still don't have a clear definition of their responsibility within their jobs. The idea that organizations can turn all of their employees into mini-entrepreneurs, and that everyone is a leader, is a misguided approach. This approach can lead to disruption because no one is sure who is handling which responsibilities. Therefore, every company needs to define its leaders and doers—which leads to the third point.

Management must provide the direction. This means not only business and market direction, but also people direction. For example, it's not uncommon for three different positions to be responsible for the same task. In the event of a crisis, however, no one claims responsibility, which leads to blaming and finger pointing. Consequently, managers need to be decisive and must take responsibility for guiding the system, much like the conductor of an orchestra leads talented, creative people through the interpretation of musical scores.

Finally, managers must use the information that comes from this well-orchestrated system to determine where changes and improvements need to be made. The most important point is that management must take action. Without analysis and action, the system will remain open-ended, and problems will continue to occur even though the system has been defined.

In summary, organizations that adopt process or systems thinking can effectively adapt to changing markets and competitive conditions, share best practices across all levels, and implement continuous improvement efforts. This systems view of organizations shows the interactions and the sequence of business activities between customers and organizational functions. The personnel understand what their responsibilities are, where they fit into the process, and how their performance affects the entire system. With clearly established roles and responsibilities, organizations can link performance results with their processes.

Chapter 3

Comparing ISO 9001:1994 with ISO 9001:2000

Users of ISO 9000 are very familiar with the numbering scheme and structure of the 1994 version. This chapter shows a comparison of ISO 9001:1994's requirements to ISO 9001:2000 by using the 1994 version's 4.1–4.20 clause structure. It's arranged in an easy-to-follow format for quick reference. Each section, by clause, includes:

■ *1994 Requirements*—a paraphrase of ISO 9001:1994's requirements

■ *What's New*—clarifications and an explanation of ISO 9001:2000's new requirements, broken down by the new numbering scheme, 4–8. The reference to the appropriate ISO 9001:2000 section is listed in parentheses.

■ *What's the Same*—a list of requirements that are the same in ISO 9001:1994 and ISO 9001:2000

■ *What's Not Included*—a list of ISO 9001:1994's requirements that are not included in ISO 9001:2000. Even when a requirement from ISO 9001:1994 is no longer explicitly stated, it's possible that auditors may still expect organizations to preserve that aspect of their quality management system.

■ *In a Nutshell*—a summary of the changes as they apply to each of ISO 9001:1994's clauses

4.1 MANAGEMENT RESPONSIBILITY

1994 REQUIREMENTS

■ Top management must define and document the organization's quality policy, quality objectives, and commitment to quality.

■ The quality policy must be relevant to the organization's goals as well as the customers' needs and expectations.

■ The quality policy must be understood, implemented, and maintained at all levels of the organization.

■ The responsibility, the authority, and the interrelation of all personnel that affect quality must be defined and documented for those personnel who need the organizational freedom to initiate action to prevent nonconformities; to identify and record problems; to initiate, recommend, and provide solutions; to verify the implementation of solutions; and to control processes until the nonconformity has been corrected.

■ Top management must identify and provide resources, including trained personnel, for management, for carrying out work activities, and for verification activities, including audits.

■ Top management must appoint a management representative who has the defined authority to:
   • ensure that the quality system is established, implemented, and maintained in accordance with the standard.
   • report on the quality system performance during the management review and use the results as a basis for improvement.

■ Top management must review the quality system at defined intervals.

■ Top management must ensure the suitability and effectiveness of the quality system related to the standard and stated quality policy and objectives.

■ The management reviews must be recorded and the records maintained.

4.1 MANAGEMENT RESPONSIBILITY

WHAT'S NEW

5 Management responsibility
Clarifications
■ It's more explicitly stated that management must establish the quality policy and quality objectives. The management review should be used to evaluate the need for changes to the quality management system, quality policy, and quality objectives. *(Reference 5.1 Management commitment; 5.6.1 General)*
■ The quality policy must be communicated and understood within the organization rather than implemented and maintained. *(Reference 5.3 Quality policy)*
■ Top management has the responsibility for and must provide evidence of their commitment to ensure the availability of resources and information. *(Reference 4.1 General requirements; 5.1 Management commitment)*
■ Top management must define responsibilities and authorities and communicate them within the organization. *(Reference 5.5.1 Responsibility and authority)*

New Requirements
■ Top management must provide evidence of their commitment to system development and ongoing improvement of its effectiveness, which includes communicating to the organization the importance of meeting customer, regulatory, and statutory requirements. *(Reference 5.1 Management commitment)*
■ Top management must ensure that customer requirements are determined and met with the aim of enhancing customer satisfaction. *(Reference 5.2 Customer focus)*
■ Top management must ensure that the quality policy:
  • includes a commitment to meeting requirements and continual improvement
  • provides framework for quality objectives
  • is reviewed for ongoing suitability
    (Reference 5.3 Quality policy)

4.1 MANAGEMENT RESPONSIBILITY

■ Quality objectives must be established at relevant functions and levels. They must be measurable and consistent with the quality policy. Objectives must include those needed to meet product requirements. *(Reference 5.4.1 Quality objectives; 7.1 Planning of product realization).*

■ Planning must be performed to meet quality objectives and requirements in section 4.1 General *(Reference 5.4.2 Quality management system planning)*

■ The integrity of the quality management system must be maintained when changes are planned and made to the system. *(Reference 5.4.2 Quality management system planning)*

■ The management representative has the authority and responsibility to promote the awareness of customer requirements throughout the organization. *(Reference 5.5.2 Management representative)*

■ Top management must ensure that processes for communication are established and that communication takes place within the organization regarding the effectiveness of the quality management system and the related processes. *(Reference 5.5.3 Internal communication)*

■ Management reviews must cover specific inputs and outputs during the review. The management review must also include assessing opportunities for improvement and evaluating any changes that could affect the quality management system, including the quality policy and quality objectives. *(Reference 5.6.1 General)*

■ Inputs to the management review must include:
- audit results
- feedback from customers
- analyses of process performance and product conformance
- preventive and corrective actions status
- follow-up actions from previous management reviews
- changes that might affect the quality management system
- improvement recommendations

(Reference 5.6.2 Review input)

4.1 MANAGEMENT RESPONSIBILITY

■ Outputs of the management review must include decisions and actions relating to:
  • the quality management system (and its processes) improvement
  • product improvement (related to customer requirements)
  • resource needs
  (Reference 5.6.3 Review output)

6 Resource management
Clarifications
■ Record-keeping requirements have been expanded to include education, training, skills, and experience. *(Reference 6.2.2 Competence, awareness, and training)*

New Requirements
■ Organizations must determine and provide the resources necessary to implement and improve the effectiveness of the quality management system and to enhance customer satisfaction. *(Reference 6.1 Provision of resources)*
■ Organizations must ensure that personnel who perform work that affects product quality are competent as well as determine what defines this competence. *(Reference 6.2.1 General; 6.2.2 Competence, awareness, and training)*

7 Product realization
Clarifications
■ Organizations must determine quality objectives and requirements that are specific to the product as appropriate. *(Reference 7.1 Planning of product realization)*

New Requirements
■ None

4.1 MANAGEMENT RESPONSIBILITY

8 Measurement, analysis, and improvement
Clarifications
■ None

New Requirements
■ The organization must plan and implement the monitoring, measurement, analysis, and continual improvement processes to ensure conformity of product, conformity of the quality management system and achieve improvement of the QMS. *(Reference 8.1 General)*
■ The standard is more specific in its requirements for attaining improvement. Organizations must facilitate continual improvements through the use of the quality policy, quality objectives, audit results, data analysis, corrective/preventive action, and management review. *(Reference 8.5.1 Continual improvement)*

WHAT'S THE SAME
■ Organizations must establish and document a quality policy and quality objectives and their commitment to them.
■ The quality policy must be relevant to organizational goals and customer requirements.
■ The quality policy must be disseminated throughout the organization.
■ Responsibilities and authorities must be defined and communicated.
■ Top management must allocate adequate resources to the quality management system.
■ The management representative must be a member of management who has defined responsibility and authority on matters relating to the quality system.
■ Top management is responsible for the periodic quality system review to ensure its suitability and effectiveness.
■ Management review records must be kept.

WHAT'S NOT INCLUDED
■ The specific list of actions for personnel who affect quality is no longer listed in ISO 9001:2000.

4.1 MANAGEMENT RESPONSIBILITY

■ Responsibility and authority for personnel "that affect quality" has been removed.

■ The specific language regarding types of resources (i.e., trained personnel) for management, for performance of work, and for verification activities, including audits, has been removed.

IN A NUTSHELL

Top management is responsible for all aspects of defining, documenting, and communicating the organization's quality policy. The quality policy must demonstrate management's "commitment" to meeting requirements and continual improvement. ISO 9001:2000 ensures that there is alignment between the quality policy, the quality objectives, and the organizational and customer requirements.

The specific activities of personnel have been eliminated from the responsibility and authority clause (ISO 9001:1994 4.1.2.1). Therefore, organizations will need to clearly define and communicate what responsibilities and authorities are necessary. ISO 9001:2000 has reduced the scope of this requirement, thus allowing organizations to become more flexible in defining who does what within the quality management system.

Top management has the ultimate responsibility for ensuring that adequate resources are provided throughout the organization to effectively implement and improve the organization's quality management system. The organization must ensure that personnel are competent based on their education, training, skills, and experience. Furthermore, the organization must determine and provide resources to implement and improve the quality management system and to enhance customer satisfaction.

The management representative now has the additional responsibility of promoting the awareness of customer requirements throughout the organization. It is up to the organization to determine how the management representative will "promote" this awareness.

4.1 MANAGEMENT RESPONSIBILITY

The purpose of the management review process is to periodically evaluate the performance and effectiveness of the quality management system. The main intent of these reviews is to determine the health of the quality management system by identifying opportunities for improvement and determining actions to facilitate the improvement. ISO 9001:2000 specifies inputs and outputs to the management review process, including evaluating changes that could affect the quality system. Furthermore, it directly links the management review process to the continual improvement of the organization.

4.2 QUALITY SYSTEM

1994 REQUIREMENTS

■ A documented quality system must be developed by creating and documenting quality procedures and work instructions and effectively implementing them.

■ The quality manual must make reference to all the documented quality system procedures relating to the ISO 9001 requirements and include an outline of the structure of the documentation used.

■ Organizations must effectively implement the quality system and its procedures.

■ Organizations must define and document how they meet their quality requirements.

■ Quality planning must be in accordance with the organizations' specifications for their products, projects, or contracts.

WHAT'S NEW

4 Quality management system

Clarifications

■ ISO 9001:2000 requires the establishment, documentation, implementation, maintenance, and continual improvement of the effectiveness of the organization's quality management system. *(Reference 4.1 General requirements)*

■ Organizations must establish and implement documentation (other than that required by ISO 9001:2000) for the effective planning, operation, and control of their processes. *(Reference 4.2.1 General)*

■ Note: The range and extent of the quality management system procedures depend on:
  • the organization's size and type
  • the complexity and interaction of the organization's processes
  • the competence of the organization's personnel
  (Reference Note under 4.2.1 General)

4.2 QUALITY SYSTEM

New Requirements
■ ISO 9001:2000 is more specific about what organizations must consider when implementing their quality management system. In order to implement a quality management system, organizations must:
- identify processes
- determine process sequence and interaction
- establish the criteria and methods necessary to ensure effective operation and control of processes
- ensure resources and information availability necessary to support processes
- measure, monitor, and analyze processes
- implement actions to achieve planned results and continual improvement
- identify the control of outsourced processes as applicable

(Reference 4.1 General requirements)

5 Management responsibility
Clarifications
■ Quality manuals must include the scope of the quality management system, including exclusions, the documented procedures (or a reference to them), and the description for the interaction of processes. *(Reference 4.2.2 Quality manual)*
■ Quality manuals must be controlled. *(Reference 4.2.1 General; 4.2.3 Control of documents)*

New Requirements
■ Quality planning includes the following items:
- Planning must be performed to meet quality objectives and requirements in section 4.1 General. *(Reference 5.4.2 Quality management system planning)*
- The integrity of the quality management system must be maintained when changes are planned and made to the system. *(Reference 5.4.2 Quality management system planning)*

4.2 QUALITY SYSTEM

6 Resource management
Clarifications
■ None

New Requirements
■ None

7 Product realization
Clarifications
■ When planning realization processes, organizations must determine the following, as appropriate:
- quality objectives and requirements for the product
- establishment of processes, documentation, and resources
- records necessary to provide confidence of conformance
- required activities specific to the product and the criteria for product acceptance

(Reference 7.1 Planning of product realization)

New Requirements
■ None

8 Measurement, analysis, and improvement
Clarifications
■ None

New Requirements
■ None

What's the Same
■ Organizations must implement a quality management system.
■ Organizations must document their quality management system with procedures defined in a quality manual.
■ Organizations must prepare documented procedures consistent with the standard.

4.2 QUALITY SYSTEM

WHAT'S NOT INCLUDED
■ An outline of the documentation structure is no longer specified.
■ As listed in 4.2.3 Quality Planning, the activities related to quality planning that were to be considered are no longer listed.

IN A NUTSHELL
The general intent for this section is the same as the 1994 version's clause 4.2; however, ISO 9001:2000 introduces the word "process." This introduction implies the use of a process-management approach for the organization. Throughout ISO 9001:2000, it's stated that processes are created to manage the ISO 9001 requirements. The new process-based structure of the standard is consistent with the Plan-Do-Check-Act improvement cycle. Under 4.2 Documentation requirements, Note 1 states that a procedure must be established, documented, implemented, and maintained where the words "documented procedure" appear in ISO 9001:2000 *(see Chapter 5, Transition Planning)*.

In the 1994 version, confusion existed around quality planning and quality plans. The revised standard has given more specific guidelines for planning and has more clearly described "quality plans" in a note under 7.1 Planning of product realization.

Organizations are required to have documented quality planning activities. The outputs from these activities form the foundation for the organizational processes needed to meet the established quality objectives. ISO 9001:2000 doesn't give a list of items to consider as appropriate. Instead, under 5.4.2 Quality management system planning, the standard lists two areas that organizational planning must cover. A new requirement specifies that the integrity of the quality management system must be maintained when changes are planned and implemented. Through this quality planning, organizations create a path to attain the desired results.

4.3 CONTRACT REVIEW

1994 REQUIREMENTS
■ Organizations must document procedures for contract review.
■ Customer requirements must be defined and documented.
■ Organizations must review contracts prior to acceptance to ensure that there are clear requirements, that any differences are resolved, and that the order requirements can be met.
■ Orders received orally must have requirements agreed upon before acceptance.
■ Organizations must determine how contract amendments are handled and how this amended information is disseminated to the correct personnel.
■ Contract review records must be maintained.

WHAT'S NEW

5 Management responsibility
Clarifications
■ None

New Requirements
■ Top management must ensure that customer requirements are defined and the requirements are met to enhance customer satisfaction. *(Reference 5.2 Customer focus)*

6 Resource management
Clarifications
■ None

New Requirements
■ None

7 Product realization
Clarifications
■ The results of the review and actions must be recorded and maintained. *(Reference 7.2.2 Review of requirements related to the product)*

4.3 CONTRACT REVIEW

■ Relevant documentation must be amended when changes occur. *(Reference 7.2.2 Review of requirements related to the product)*

New Requirements
■ Defining the customer requirements has been expanded to include requirements for delivery and post-delivery activities as well as regulatory and statutory requirements. *(Reference 7.2.1 Determination of requirements related to the product)*
■ Organizations must identify and implement arrangements for customer communication relating to product information, order handling, and customer feedback, including complaints. *(Reference 7.2.3 Customer communication)*

8 Measurement, analysis, and improvement
Clarifications
■ None

New Requirements
■ None

WHAT'S THE SAME
■ Organizations must review contracts prior to order acceptance to ensure the requirements are clearly defined, that requirements can be met, and that any differences are resolved prior to acceptance.
■ Contract amendment information must be disseminated to the correct personnel.
■ Contract review records must be maintained.

WHAT'S NOT INCLUDED
■ Documented procedures for contract review are no longer specifically stated.

4.3 CONTRACT REVIEW

IN A NUTSHELL

The ISO 9001:2000 contract review requirements are basically the same as in ISO 9001:1994. Some of the wording has changed; however, the general intent is the same. The new standard has expanded the idea of contract review. Organizations must determine customer requirements, identify and implement arrangements for customer communication, and convert these requirements into products and/or services that will enhance customer satisfaction. More information on this topic can be found in Chapter 4, Noteworthy Changes.

4.4 DESIGN CONTROL

1994 Requirements

■ Organizations must maintain procedures that control and verify product designs to ensure that they meet specified requirements.

■ Organizations must develop plans for design activity that designate the personnel responsible for implementation. The responsible personnel must be qualified and have adequate resources.

■ The design plans must be updated as the design evolves.

■ Defined organizational and technical interfaces must exist that document, transmit, and regularly review necessary information.

■ The design-input activities must be identified, documented, and reviewed for adequacy.

■ Responsible personnel must resolve any conflicts or ambiguities in the input requirements.

■ Organizations must consider the results of contract review activities as design input.

■ Design-output must be documented in terms that are verified and validated against design-input requirements.

■ The design output must meet design-input requirements, contain or reference acceptance criteria, identify critical product characteristics, and be reviewed prior to release.

■ Pertinent personnel must plan and conduct formal documented reviews and maintain records of the reviews.

■ Organizations must conduct design verification to ensure design-stage output meets the design-stage input requirements.

■ Design verification measures must be recorded.

■ Organizations must conduct design validation to ensure that the product conforms to defined user needs/requirements.

■ Changes and modifications throughout the design process must be identified, documented, reviewed, and approved before implementation.

What's New

5 Management responsibility
Clarifications
■ None

4.4 DESIGN CONTROL

New Requirements
■ None

6 Resource management
Clarifications
■ None

New Requirements
■ None

7 Product realization
Clarifications
■ The interfaces between different groups must be "managed" to ensure effective communication and clarity of responsibilities. *(Reference 7.3.1 Design and development planning)*
■ Planning requirements are more specific and require that the design and development planning determine the review (7.3.4), verification (7.3.5), and validation (7.3.6) appropriate at each stage. These activities must be performed in accordance with planned arrangements. *(Reference 7.3.1 Design and development planning)*
■ The results of the review and necessary actions must be recorded and maintained. *(Reference 7.3.4 Design and development review)*
■ The results of verification and necessary actions must be recorded and maintained. *(Reference 7.3.5 Design and development verification)*
■ The results of the review of changes and necessary actions must be recorded and maintained. *(Reference 7.3.7 Control of design and development changes)*

New Requirements
■ Design and development input requirements must include functional and performance requirements, requirements derived from previous similar designs, and any other requirements essential for design and development. *(Reference 7.3.2 Design and development inputs)*

4.4 DESIGN CONTROL

■ Design and development outputs must provide relevant information for purchasing, production, and service provision. *(Reference 7.3.3 Design and development outputs)*

■ The design and development reviews must be conducted to evaluate the capability to meet requirements, to identify any problems, and to propose necessary actions. *(Reference 7.3.4 Design and development review)*

■ Where practical, the validation must be completed prior to delivery or implementation of the product. Validation results and necessary actions must be recorded and maintained. *(Reference 7.3.6 Design and development validation)*

■ Organizations must determine the effect of the changes on the constituent parts and delivered products. As appropriate, the changes must be reviewed, verified, and validated before implementation. *(Reference 7.3.7 Control of design and development changes)*

8 Measurement, analysis, and improvement
Clarifications
■ None

New Requirements
■ None

WHAT'S THE SAME
■ Organizations must plan and control the design and development of a product or service.

■ Design input information must be reviewed for adequacy, and conflicting requirements must be resolved.

■ Design output must be documented in terms that can be verified and validated against design-input requirements.

■ The design output must meet design-input requirements, contain or reference acceptance criteria, identify critical product characteristics, and be reviewed prior to release.

■ Pertinent personnel must plan and conduct formal documented reviews and maintain records of the reviews.

4.4 DESIGN CONTROL

■ Organizations must conduct design and development verification to ensure that design-stage output meets the design-stage input requirements.

■ Organizations must conduct design and development validation to ensure the product conforms to intended customer use.

■ Changes and modifications throughout the design and development process must be documented and approved before implementation.

WHAT'S NOT INCLUDED

■ The 1994 requirement to define interfaces between different groups is no longer specified.

■ A procedure for design control is no longer specified.

IN A NUTSHELL

The main purpose of each of the subclauses of the 1994 version of 4.4 Design Control has been addressed in ISO 9001:2000. Additional requirements have been added to further ensure that organizations clearly understand what their customer requirements are before they begin the design process. For example, the design input and output requirements are more specifically stated. Organizations will be required to consider the effect of design changes on several items. Furthermore, the results of these changes and any associated actions must be documented.

4.5 DOCUMENT AND DATA CONTROL

1994 REQUIREMENTS

■ Organizations must maintain procedures for controlling quality system documentation and data, which include external documents.

■ Documents and data must be reviewed and approved for adequacy. A master list or similar tool must be established to ensure revision control and to prevent the inadvertent use of obsolete documents.

■ Pertinent issues of documents must be available.

■ Invalid or obsolete documents must be promptly removed.

■ Obsolete documents that are retained must be identified.

■ Document and data changes must be reviewed and approved by the same personnel that performed the original review and approval.

■ Where practical, the nature of the change must be identified.

WHAT'S NEW

4 Quality management system
Clarifications

■ The control of external documents must include the identification and distribution of these documents. *(Reference 4.2.3 Control of documents)*

New Requirements

■ The procedure for the control of documents must include a provision for ensuring that documents remain legible and readily identifiable. *(Reference 4.2.3 Control of documents)*

■ Documents defined as records must be controlled. *(Reference 4.2.3 Control of documents)*

5 Management responsibility
Clarifications

■ None

New Requirements

■ None

4.5 DOCUMENT AND DATA CONTROL

6 Resource management
Clarifications
■ None

New Requirements
■ None

7 Product realization
Clarifications
■ None

New Requirements
■ None

8 Measurement, analysis, and improvement
Clarifications
■ None

New Requirements
■ None

WHAT'S THE SAME
■ Organizations must maintain documented procedures for controlling quality system documentation, including external documents.
■ Organizations must be able to identify current revision status of documents.
■ Documents must be approved for adequacy prior to release. Revision control must be used to prevent the inadvertent use of obsolete documents.
■ Obsolete documents must be identified, if retained.
■ Documents must be reviewed, updated as necessary, and re-approved.
■ The note in the 1994 version including all types of media is now found in Note 3 in 4.2.1 General.

4.5 DOCUMENT AND DATA CONTROL

WHAT'S NOT INCLUDED

■ The requirement that document and data changes must be reviewed and approved by the same personnel that performed the original review and approval is no longer specified.

■ It's no longer specified that the nature of the changes must be identified within the document or appropriate attachments.

■ The specific reference to a master list has been removed.

IN A NUTSHELL

There are no significant changes regarding document control. The main intent of the 1994 version's 4.5 Document and Data Control is included, except that the word "data" has been omitted. However, the control of data is implied because documents defined as records must be controlled. In ISO 9001:2000, an organization must identify the current revision of a document, although it does not specify how it needs to be done (e.g., master list).

4.6 PURCHASING

1994 REQUIREMENTS

■ Organizations must maintain procedures to ensure that purchased product conforms to specified requirements.

■ Subcontractors must be selected and evaluated based on their ability to meet quality system requirements.

■ The extent and control over subcontractors must be based on product type, quality impact on the final product, and demonstrated capability.

■ Records of acceptable subcontractors must be maintained.

■ Purchasing documents must clearly describe the product that is ordered and must be reviewed and approved prior to release.

■ Organizations may verify purchased product at a subcontractor location after verification arrangements and the product release method have been specified.

■ Customers may verify purchased product at the organization's subcontractor location if contractually specified. In this case, organizations are still responsible for providing acceptable products to their customers.

WHAT'S NEW

4 Quality management system
Clarifications
■ None

New Requirements
■ Where processes that affect product quality are outsourced, organizations must identify and control these processes. *(Reference 4.1 General requirements)*

5 Management responsibility
Clarifications
■ None

4.6 PURCHASING

New Requirements
- None

6 Resource management
Clarifications
- None

New Requirements
- None

7 Product realization
Clarifications
- In order to eliminate confusion caused in the 1994 edition, the term "supplier" has replaced the term "subcontractor" and the term "organization" has replaced the term "supplier." *(Reference 3 Terms and definitions)*
- Organizations must establish the criteria upon which suppliers will be selected, evaluated, and re-evaluated. The results of these evaluations and any necessary actions must be maintained. *(Reference 7.4.1 Purchasing process)*
- The "review and approval" requirement of purchasing documents prior to release has been replaced by a requirement for "ensuring the adequacy" of purchasing documents prior to release. *(Reference 7.4.2 Purchasing information)*
- There is now one joint requirement for the organization or customer verification of purchased product at a supplier's location. Verification arrangements and the method of product release are still required in purchasing documents. *(Reference 7.4.3 Verification of purchased product)*

New Requirements
- None

4.6 PURCHASING

8 Measurement, analysis, and improvement
Clarifications
■ None

New Requirements
■ None

WHAT'S THE SAME
■ Organizations must maintain purchasing processes to ensure that purchased product conforms to specified requirements.
■ Subcontractors must be selected and evaluated based on their ability to supply product and/or service in accordance with organizational requirements. Records of subcontractor activity must be maintained.
■ The extent and control over subcontractors must be based on the quality impact on the final product.
■ Purchasing documents must clearly describe the product that is ordered and must be reviewed prior to release.
■ Organizations or their customers may verify purchased product at a subcontractor location after verification arrangements and the product release method have been specified.

WHAT'S NOT INCLUDED
■ The paragraph that describes, where applicable, purchasing data, including type, class, grade, or other product identification; title or positive identification; applicable specifications; drawings; process requirements; inspection instructions; and other relevant technical data has been removed.
■ Basing the control of subcontractors on the type of product, the subcontractor's previously demonstrated capability, and audit records and reports is no longer specified.
■ The customer's verification of a subcontractor does not pardon the organization from the responsibility to provide acceptable product, is no longer a requirement.
■ A procedure for purchasing is no longer specified.

4.6 PURCHASING

IN A NUTSHELL

The purpose of ISO 9001:1994's 4.6 Purchasing has remained the same; however, the section focused on control over suppliers has been modified. The terminology has been improved to eliminate confusion surrounding the terms "subcontractor" and "supplier." Several of the items that were required "where applicable" on purchasing documents have been eliminated. Organizations will still need to consider what criteria they use for supplier selection and how often their suppliers should be evaluated. Overall, the purchasing section still focuses on ensuring that purchased product conforms to specifications and that purchasing documents clearly describe what is being ordered.

4.7 CONTROL OF CUSTOMER-SUPPLIED PRODUCT

1994 REQUIREMENTS
■ Organizations must have procedures for how they control products supplied by their customers for incorporation into the organizations' products.
■ Organizations are responsible for the proper maintenance, control of verification, and storage of their customers' products.
■ Organizations must record and report lost, damaged, or unsuitable customer-supplied products to their customers.
■ Although organizations must verify customer-supplied products, the customer is still responsible for providing acceptable products.

WHAT'S NEW

5 Management responsibility
Clarifications
■ None

New Requirements
■ None

6 Resource management
Clarifications
■ None

New Requirements
■ None

7 Product realization
Clarifications
■ The terminology now used is to "exercise care" with customer property while it is under the organization's control or in use by the organization. *(Reference 7.5.4 Customer property)*
■ Organizations must "identify, verify, protect, and safeguard" customer property. *(Reference 7.5.4 Customer property)*

4.7 CONTROL OF CUSTOMER-SUPPLIED PRODUCT

■ The note in this section states that customer property may also include property of an intellectual nature, which is defined as information provided to organizations by customers in confidence. *(Reference 7.5.4 Customer property)*

New Requirements
■ None

8 Measurement, analysis, and improvement
Clarifications
■ None

New Requirements
■ None

WHAT'S THE SAME
■ Organizations are responsible for the proper maintenance and storage of customer-supplied product, and any damage must be documented and reported to their customers.

WHAT'S NOT INCLUDED
■ A documented procedure for customer-supplied products is no longer specified.

IN A NUTSHELL
There are no significant changes in this section. The words "identify and protect" have been added to the requirements for clarification. Organizations are still completely responsible when handling customer property. Any problems with the customer's property are documented and the customer is notified. The term "property" is now used in place of "product."

4.8 PRODUCT IDENTIFICATION AND TRACEABILITY

1994 REQUIREMENTS

■ Where applicable, organizations must maintain documented procedures for the suitable identification of product from receipt through production, delivery, and installation.

■ If required in a customer contract, organizations must maintain documented procedures for the unique identification of individual product and batches. The unique identification must be recorded.

WHAT'S NEW

5 Management responsibility
Clarifications
■ None

New Requirements
■ None

6 Resource management
Clarifications
■ None

New Requirements
■ None

7 Product realization
Clarifications
■ The 4.12 Inspection and Test Status requirement has been included in this section. The intent remains the same, although the description of the requirement has been reduced significantly. *(Reference 7.5.3 Identification and traceability)*
■ Organizations must not only record the unique identification but also control it. *(Reference 7.5.3 Identification and traceability)*

New Requirements
■ None

4.8 PRODUCT IDENTIFICATION AND TRACEABILITY

8 Measurement, analysis, and improvement
Clarifications
■ None

New Requirements
■ None

What's the Same
■ Where applicable, organizations must suitably identify products throughout production and service operations.
■ The unique identification number must be recorded where traceability is a requirement.

What's Not Included
■ The requirement to establish documented procedures for identifying products is no longer specified.
■ The specified requirement for documented procedures in relation to unique identification of individual product and batches has been removed.

In a Nutshell
In ISO 9001:2000, the 1994 version's 4.8 Product Identification and Traceability and 4.12 Inspection and Test Status are combined under one section. The intent is that organizations will use these requirements, as applicable, for their processes.

4.9 PROCESS CONTROL

1994 REQUIREMENTS

■ Organizations must identify and plan the production, installation, and servicing processes that directly affect quality and ensure that these processes are carried out under controlled conditions.

■ Organizations must provide documented work instructions and specify workmanship criteria.

■ Organizations must use, maintain, and approve suitable equipment and provide a suitable working environment.

■ Organizations must monitor and control process parameters and product characteristics.

■ Organizations must remain in compliance with reference standards/codes, quality plans, and documented procedures.

■ For special processes, organizations must use qualified personnel and maintain records for qualified processes, equipment, and personnel.

WHAT'S NEW

5 Management responsibility
Clarifications
■ None

New Requirements
■ None

6 Resource management
Clarifications
■ None

New Requirements
■ Organizations must identify, provide, and maintain the infrastructure necessary to achieve conformity of their products. *(Reference 6.3 Infrastructure)*

■ Organizations must determine and manage the work environment needed for product conformity. *(Reference 6.4 Work environment)*

4.9 PROCESS CONTROL

7 Product realization

Clarifications

■ Organizations must plan and develop the processes that will result in product realization. Note 1 states that the quality plan consists of the documentation that specifies these processes within the quality management system. *(Reference 7.1 Planning of product realization)*

■ More specific requirements are listed for establishing arrangements, as applicable, for special processes. *(Reference 7.5.2 Validation of processes for production and service provision)*

■ Documented procedures defining the manner of production, installation, and servicing has been changed to availability of work instructions as necessary. *(Reference 7.5.1 Control of production and service provision)*

New Requirements

■ Organizations must have available the information that defines the characteristics of the products that are to be achieved, as applicable. *(Reference 7.5.1 Control of production and service provision)*

■ "Special processes" must be validated and revalidated, as applicable, to demonstrate the ability of the processes to achieve planned results. *(Reference 7.5.2 Validation of processes for production and service provision)*

8 Measurement, analysis, and improvement

Clarifications

■ None

New Requirements

■ None

WHAT'S THE SAME

■ Organizations must plan and control their production and service operations.

■ Processes must be monitored.

■ Organizations must use suitable equipment.

4.9 PROCESS CONTROL

■ For special processes, organizations must use qualified personnel and maintain records for qualified processes, equipment, and personnel.

WHAT'S NOT INCLUDED
■ Controlled conditions that are no longer referenced include:
- criteria for workmanship
- approval of processes and equipment, as appropriate
- compliance with reference standards/codes, quality plans, and documented procedures
- suitable maintenance of equipment to ensure process capability

IN A NUTSHELL
Section 7.5 Production and service provision incorporates some of the requirements of the ISO 9001:1994 clauses, such as 4.19 Servicing, as well as most of the requirements of 4.9 Process Control. Organizations are still required to maintain operations in a controlled environment and provide work instructions for personnel (where necessary). There are several new requirements, however, that expand on some of the basic requirements in the 1994 version. Organizations must now consider how they validate and revalidate special processes where the resulting output cannot be verified by subsequent measuring. They also must consider the infrastructure (6.3) and work environment (6.4) *(see Chapter 4, Noteworthy Changes)*.

Even though a specific reference to maintenance of equipment is no longer included, it is implied in 6.3 Infrastructure.

4.10 INSPECTION AND TESTING

1994 REQUIREMENTS

■ Organizations must maintain procedures for inspection and testing activities to ensure that products conform to specified requirements.

■ Organizations must inspect or verify incoming product conformance to specifications prior to being used.

■ Organizations must determine the amount of required receiving inspection based on the control of suppliers as well as documented evidence of specification conformance.

■ Organizations must positively identify any product released for urgent production in the event of recall.

■ Organizations must inspect and test all in-process products per the documented procedures, and no product is to be released until all inspection and test activities have been performed successfully.

■ Organizations must ensure that all final inspection and testing is conducted in accordance with documented procedures. These procedures require that all incoming and in-process tests were completed.

■ Product is to be released only after all activities specified in the documented procedures are completed and the data and documentation is available and authorized.

■ Organizations must maintain records to show that their products have been inspected. The records must show that the products either passed or failed. Records must identify who is responsible for releasing products.

WHAT'S NEW

5 Management responsibility

Clarifications
■ None

New Requirements
■ None

4.10 INSPECTION AND TESTING

6 Resource management
Clarifications
- None

New Requirements
- None

7 Product realization
Clarifications
- The terminology "inspection and testing" has now been changed to "monitoring and measurement." Organizations are responsible for implementing monitoring activities *(Reference 7.5.1 Control of production and service provision)*, determining verification and validation activities, and establishing the criteria for acceptability *(Reference 7.1 Planning of product realization)*.
- Organizations must define and implement processes for release, delivery, and post-delivery activities. This is a combination of 4.10 Inspection and Testing; 4.15 Handling, Storage, Packaging, Preservation, and Delivery; and 4.19 Servicing from ISO 9001:1994. *(Reference 7.5.1 Control of production and service provision)*
- Clarifies receiving inspection or activities for ensuring that purchased product meets specified purchase requirements. *(Reference 7.4.3 Verification of purchased product)*

New Requirements
- None

8 Measurement, analysis, and improvement
Clarifications
- Organizations must plan and implement measurement and monitoring activities to demonstrate conformity of product. *(Reference 8.1 General)*
- Organizations must apply methods for monitoring and measurement of the quality management system processes. The methods must ensure the ability of the process to achieve planned results. *(Reference 8.2.3 Monitoring and measurement of processes)*

4.10 INSPECTION AND TESTING

■ Organizations must measure and monitor product characteristics to ensure that requirements are met. *(Reference 8.2.4 Monitoring and measurement of product)*

New Requirements
■ None

WHAT'S THE SAME
■ The specific breakdown of inspection activities, i.e., receiving, in-process, final, and record requirements, is no longer explicit in the standard, although ISO 9001:2000 *implies* that inspection activities must be carried out.
■ Product release cannot proceed until all activities are satisfactorily carried out.
■ Organizations must document evidence of conformity with the acceptance criteria.
■ Organizations must maintain records of the authority responsible for the release of the product.

WHAT'S NOT INCLUDED
■ The specific reference to receiving, in-process, final, and inspection requirements is no longer included.
■ The requirement that records must show both pass and fail status is no longer stated—only conformity is specified.
■ The requirement for documented procedures is no longer specified.

IN A NUTSHELL
Much of ISO 9001:1994's 4.10 Inspection and Testing's text has been moved to ISO 9004:2000's sections 7.4.1 Purchasing process, 7.4.3 Verification of purchased product, and 8.2.4 Monitoring and measurement of product; however, the purpose of 4.10 has remained. Organizations are required to determine what measurement and

4.10 INSPECTION AND TESTING

monitoring methods will be employed to ensure that both process and product and/or service requirements are met. ISO 9001:2000 doesn't explicitly specify inspection and testing activities for incoming, in-process, and final product. There still must be documented evidence that products and/or services conform to specifications, and evidence must show what acceptance criteria is used. When addressing monitoring and verification requirements, it will be important to review all of the applicable sections of the revised standard to meet the requirements.

4.11 CONTROL OF INSPECTION, MEASURING, AND TEST EQUIPMENT

1994 Requirements

■ Organizations must establish and maintain documented procedures.

■ Equipment must be used in a way that ensures that measurement uncertainty is known and is consistent with required measurement capability.

■ If organizations use test software or comparative references for inspection, they must be checked for proof of capability for verification activities and rechecked at selected intervals. The extent and frequency of such checks must be determined by the organization, and records must be maintained.

■ Organizations must make technical data pertaining to measurement equipment available to their customers if necessary to determine if equipment is functioning adequately.

■ Organizations must:

• Determine measurements and accuracy required for equipment.
• Ensure that equipment is capable of measuring to the needed accuracy and precision.
• Identify all inspection, measuring, and test equipment that will affect the quality of the product.
• Ensure that their equipment is calibrated at specified intervals, or prior to use, against certified equipment traceable to international or national standards.
• Define the process for calibration, including details of equipment type, unique identification, location, frequency of checks, check method, acceptance criteria, and action to be taken when results are unsatisfactory.
• Identify equipment to show calibration status.
• Maintain records.
• Assess previous inspections for validity when equipment used is out of calibration.
• Ensure that environmental conditions are suitable for the calibrations and inspections.
• Ensure that equipment is handled, preserved, and stored to maintain accuracy and fitness for use.
• Safeguard inspection, measuring, and test facilities from adjustments that would invalidate the calibration.

4.11 CONTROL OF INSPECTION, MEASURING, AND TEST EQUIPMENT

WHAT'S NEW

5 Management responsibility
Clarifications
- None

New Requirements
- None

6 Resource management
Clarifications
- None

New Requirements
- None

7 Product realization
Clarifications
- The results of calibration and verification must be recorded and maintained. ISO 9001:1994 only stated that the calibration records for inspection, measuring, and test equipment must be maintained. *(Reference 7.6 Control of monitoring and measuring devices)*
- The control of production and service operations include the availability and use of monitoring and measuring devices. *(Reference 7.5.1 Control of production and service provision)*
- The ability of computer software to monitor and measure the intended application must be confirmed prior to use. *(Reference 7.6 Control of monitoring and measuring devices)*
- Establish processes for carrying out monitoring and measurement activities. *(Reference 7.6 Control of monitoring and measuring devices)*

New Requirements
- None

4.11 CONTROL OF INSPECTION, MEASURING, AND TEST EQUIPMENT

8 Measurement, analysis, and improvement
Clarifications
■ None

New Requirements
■ None

WHAT'S THE SAME
■ Organizations must identify measurement needs and devices to use and must also ensure that the measurement capability is consistent with the monitoring and measurement requirements.
■ Measurement devices must be calibrated against known traceable standards, or, where no standard exists, the basis for calibration must be recorded.
■ Measurement equipment must be safeguarded against adjustments that would invalidate the measurement result.
■ Measurement devices must be protected from damage and deterioration.
■ Organizations must maintain calibration records.
■ Out-of-calibration results must be reassessed for validity, and corrective action must be taken.
■ The note referencing ISO 10012 remains the same.

WHAT'S NOT INCLUDED
■ The methods for establishing and maintaining documented procedures is no longer specified.
■ The requirement that test software and hardware be rechecked at prescribed intervals and that the extent and frequency of the checks be defined is no longer specified.
■ The requirement that records be kept for the test software/hardware checks is no longer stated.
■ Specifics are no longer provided for defining the process employed for the calibration of inspection, measuring, and test equipment, including details of equipment type, unique identification, location, frequency of checks, check method, or acceptance criteria.

4.11 CONTROL OF INSPECTION, MEASURING, AND TEST EQUIPMENT

■ Requirements for suitable environmental conditions for carrying out calibrations, measurements, etc. have been removed.
■ Technical data pertaining to measurement for verification of equipment must be made available to the customer.
■ There is no longer a reference to ensuring that the measurement uncertainty is known.

IN A NUTSHELL

One significant change in the revised standard is the term "where applicable" for the specific ISO 9001:1994 a–e requirements as applied to organizations' measuring and monitoring devices. ISO 9001:2000 does not make it clear whether organizations can determine which of the requirements apply to their devices and ignore the others. This may be one of those gray areas that will require interpretation by registrars.

Another difference in ISO 9001:2000 is the elimination of a reference to test hardware. Also, the revised standard no longer specifies some of the specific requirements that some companies found helpful when setting up their systems, such as detailing equipment type, unique identification, location, and frequency and method of checks.

Finally, one other requirement is no longer included in the standard: ensuring that the environmental conditions for carrying out the calibrations, inspections, and measurement are suitable.

The fundamental purpose of ISO 9001:1994's clause 4.11 has remained the same. It's strongly suggested that these systems remain intact to preserve the same discipline and routine that was required by ISO 9001:1994.

4.12 INSPECTION AND TEST STATUS

1994 REQUIREMENTS

■ The inspection and test status of products must be identified.

■ The identification must indicate conformance or nonconformance of the product in regard to inspections and tests performed.

■ The identification must be defined in the quality plan or procedures.

■ The identification must be maintained throughout production, installation, and servicing to ensure that only conforming product is released, used, or installed.

WHAT'S NEW

5 Management responsibility

Clarifications

■ None

New Requirements

■ None

6 Resource management

Clarifications

■ None

New Requirements

■ None

7 Product realization

Clarifications

■ None

New Requirements

■ None

4.12 INSPECTION AND TEST STATUS

8 Measurement, analysis, and improvement
Clarifications
■ None

New Requirements
■ None

WHAT'S THE SAME
■ Organizations must identify the status of product as related to measurement and monitoring requirements.

WHAT'S NOT INCLUDED
■ The requirement that inspection status indicate conformance and nonconformance is no longer stated.
■ Identification of inspection and test status no longer needs to be defined in the quality plan or in a documented procedure.
■ The requirement that only product that has passed inspection is released, used, or installed is no longer specified.

IN A NUTSHELL
The inspection and test status requirements from ISO 9001:1994 are not explicitly stated in ISO 9001:2000, though the purpose of inspection status appears in 7.5.3 Identification and traceability and in 7.5.1 Control of production and service provision (implementation of release activities). It's simply a good business practice to know the inspection status of product throughout production, service, or installation to ensure that only conforming product is used, released, or installed. Organizations that practice this are advised to continue. Organizations that are considering adopting ISO 9001:2000 should carefully review their systems to ensure that they have sound product inspection and testing practices in place. These practices should clearly address conforming and nonconforming product to prevent the shipment of nonconforming product.

4.13 CONTROL OF NONCONFORMING PRODUCT

1994 REQUIREMENTS

■ Organizations must document procedures to ensure that nonconforming product is prevented from being used unintentionally. The procedures must describe methods for identification, documentation, evaluation, segregation (when possible), disposition, and communication to the appropriate parties.

■ The responsibility for review and authority for the disposition must be defined.

■ Nonconforming product must be reviewed according to documented procedures.

■ If contractually required, use or repair of nonconforming products must be reported to customers, and records must be kept describing the nonconformity and repairs.

■ Repaired and reworked product must be re-inspected according to procedures or quality plans.

WHAT'S NEW

5 Management responsibility
Clarifications
■ None

New Requirements
■ The review of product conformity is now a requirement for management review. *(Reference 5.6.2 Review input)*

6 Resource management
Clarifications
■ None

New Requirements
■ None

4.13 CONTROL OF NONCONFORMING PRODUCT

7 Product realization
Clarifications
■ None

New Requirements
■ None

8 Measurement, analysis, and improvement
Clarifications
■ Broader description for handling disposition; the requirement no longer includes terms such as "reworked," "rejected," or "scrapped." *(Reference 8.3 Control of nonconforming product)*
■ Records must include any subsequent actions taken, including concessions regarding the nonconformities. *(Reference 8.3 Control of nonconforming product)*

New Requirements
■ If organizations discover nonconforming products after delivery or after use has started, they must take action. *(Reference 8.3 Control of nonconforming product)*

WHAT'S THE SAME
■ Nonconforming products must be identified and controlled to prevent unintended use.
■ Organizations must have documented procedures for controlling nonconforming products.
■ Organizations must reverify or re-inspect repaired or reworked products.
■ The responsibility and authority for dealing with nonconforming products must be defined.
■ Nonconforming products must be reviewed in accordance with documented procedures.
■ Records describing the nonconformances must be maintained.

4.13 CONTROL OF NONCONFORMING PRODUCT

WHAT'S NOT INCLUDED

■ It is no longer specified that reverification activities be done in accordance with a quality plan or documented procedures.

■ The requirement to report nonconformances to the customer for concession *when required by contract* is no longer specified.

■ The details for control of nonconforming product (e.g., documentation, evaluation, disposition, and notification of functions concerned) are no longer included.

IN A NUTSHELL

Overall, the message of ISO 9001:1994's 4.13 Control of Nonconforming Product remains the same: Product that does not conform to specified requirements should not be used or shipped. A new requirement has been added for organizations to address nonconforming product that is detected after delivery. Specifically, organizations must take action related to the consequences of nonconformity when the nonconformance is detected after delivery or use has started.

4.14 CORRECTIVE AND PREVENTIVE ACTION

1994 REQUIREMENTS
■ Procedures for implementing corrective and preventive actions must be documented.
■ Any actions taken to eliminate cause must be appropriate for the size of the problem.
■ Any changes to documented procedures resulting from corrective or preventive actions must be recorded.
■ Procedures for corrective action must include effectively handling customer complaints and product nonconformities, investigating the cause of nonconformities (includes product, process, system), recording the results of the investigation, determining actions to be taken to eliminate actual problem, and devising methods for ensuring that the actions taken are effective.
■ Procedures for preventive action must include the use of relevant information to detect, analyze, and eliminate potential causes of problems; the steps required to implement preventive action; methods of ensuring that actions taken are effective; and evidence that information on actions taken is submitted to management review.

WHAT'S NEW

5 Management responsibility
Clarifications
■ ISO 9001:2000 now explicitly requires that the status of corrective and preventive actions be reviewed during management review. *(Reference 5.6.2 Review input)*

New Requirements
■ None

6 Resource management
Clarifications
■ None

4.14 CORRECTIVE AND PREVENTIVE ACTION

New Requirements
■ None

7 Product realization
Clarifications
■ None

New Requirements
■ Organizations must determine and implement effective methods for communicating to the customer regarding customer feedback, including complaints. *(Reference 7.2.3 Customer communication)*

8 Measurement, analysis, and improvement
Clarifications
■ The procedure for corrective action must define requirements for corrective action activities. *(Reference 8.5.2 Corrective action)*
■ Corrective action must prevent recurrence of problems and preventive actions must prevent occurrence of problems. *(Reference 8.5.2 Corrective action; 8.5.3 Preventive action)*
■ The results of the corrective action taken, instead of the results of the investigation, must be recorded. *(Reference 8.5.2 Corrective action)*
■ Actions taken must be appropriate for the problem. *(Reference 8.5.2 Corrective action; 8.5.3 Preventive action)*

New Requirements
■ Organizations must define methods for obtaining and using information relating to customer perceptions. ISO 9001:1994 only required the effective handling of customer complaints. *(Reference 8.2.1 Customer satisfaction)*
■ Organizations must continually improve the effectiveness of their quality management systems and use corrective and preventive actions as a basis for facilitating improvements. *(Reference 8.5.1 Continual improvement)*

4.14 CORRECTIVE AND PREVENTIVE ACTION

■ Organizations must now record the results of the preventive actions. *(Reference 8.5.3 Preventive action)*

WHAT'S THE SAME
■ The purpose of ISO 9001:1994's requirements has, for the most part, remained the same.
■ The requirement for documented procedures has remained.

WHAT'S NOT INCLUDED
■ The requirement to implement and record changes to the documented procedures resulting from corrective or preventive action is no longer stated.
■ The requirement for submitting preventive actions to management review has been moved to the Management Review section. *(Reference 5.6.2 Review input)*
■ The reference to "application of controls" to ensure that corrective or preventive actions are effective has been eliminated and replaced with a requirement to review and record the results of the actions taken.
■ The requirement to record the results of the investigation of corrective action has been changed; the standard now requires recording the results of the corrective action itself.
■ The references to specific sources of information (i.e., audit results, quality records, etc.) to detect, analyze, and eliminate potential causes have been removed.

IN A NUTSHELL
The discussion of corrective and preventive action in ISO 9001:1994 has been reworded rather than changed. Corrective and preventive actions are now classified as one of the tools that organizations must use to facilitate improvements. Furthermore, by requiring that the review of these actions be part of management reviews, ISO 9001:2000 clearly establishes top management's responsibility for the

4.14 CORRECTIVE AND PREVENTIVE ACTION

improvement of the organization. It also states that actions taken must prevent recurrence. When reviewing actions taken over time, organizations must also ensure that repeat occurrences are addressed.

Due to the greater emphasis on documenting the results of corrective and preventive actions, organizations should consider what format will be the easiest to use and understand. Many organizations document the problem-solving steps involved for the investigation of nonconformities using some type of methodology. Typically, this methodology includes problem identification, root-cause analysis, determination and implementation of corrective and preventive actions, follow-up, and closure. This information is documented and considered a quality record, which should be submitted in a summary format for management review.

4.15 HANDLING, STORAGE, PACKAGING, PRESERVATION, AND DELIVERY

1994 REQUIREMENTS

■ Organizations must have documented procedures for handling, storage, packaging, preservation, and delivery.

■ Organizations must provide methods for handling product to prevent damage and deterioration.

■ Organizations must use designated storage areas or stock rooms to prevent damage/deterioration of product prior to delivery.

■ Methods must be in place for receiving and removing product from storage areas.

■ The condition of product in storage must be assessed at regular intervals.

■ Organizations must control their packing, packaging, and marking processes, including the materials used to ensure that their customers' needs are met.

■ Appropriate methods of preserving and segregating the product must be applied.

■ Organizations must arrange for the protection of the product after final inspection and testing. If contractually agreed upon, the protection must extend to delivery of product to the final destination.

WHAT'S NEW

5 Management responsibility
Clarifications
■ None

New Requirements
■ None

6 Resource management
Clarifications
■ None

New Requirements
■ None

4.15 HANDLING, STORAGE, PACKAGING, PRESERVATION, AND DELIVERY

7 Product realization

Clarifications

■ Organizations must ensure that conformity of product be preserved from internal processing through final delivery. This must include identification, handling, storage, packaging, and protection of product. *(Reference 7.5.5 Preservation of product)*

■ ISO 9001:1994 stated that when contractually specified, protection of product must be extended to include delivery to destination. ISO 9001:2000 now requires the implementation of controlled conditions. *(Reference 7.5.1 Control of production and service provision)*

New Requirements

■ The requirement extends to constituent parts of a product. *(Reference 7.5.5 Preservation of product)*

8 Measurement, analysis, and improvement

Clarifications

■ None

New Requirements

■ None

WHAT'S THE SAME

■ A system must be in place to ensure that the product or service is not affected during internal processing and final delivery.

WHAT'S NOT INCLUDED

■ The requirement for documented procedures is not explicit for handling, storage, packaging, preservation, and delivery. It is implied under 7.5.1 Control of production and service provision, which references controlled conditions and work instructions.

■ The methods for handling product to prevent damage and deterioration are not specifically stated.

4.15 HANDLING, STORAGE, PACKAGING, PRESERVATION, AND DELIVERY

■ The requirement to use designated storage areas or stock rooms to prevent damage/deterioration of product prior to delivery is no longer specified.

■ The methods for receiving and removing product from storage areas are not specifically stated.

■ The requirement that the condition of products in storage be assessed at regular intervals is no longer stated.

■ The requirement for organizations to control packing, packaging, and marking processes, including the materials used to ensure that their customers' needs are met, has been removed.

■ The requirement for organizations to apply appropriate methods of preserving and segregating products is no longer specified.

IN A NUTSHELL

The requirements for handling, storage, packaging, preservation, and delivery have been considerably broadened. The user is advised to read the corresponding section in ISO 9004:2000 when developing a quality management system, especially the section concerning handling, storage, packaging, preservation, and delivery. Because the specific requirements have been reduced, it will be important for organizations to consider best practices for packaging, warehousing, and material handling when addressing these requirements.

4.16 CONTROL OF QUALITY RECORDS

1994 REQUIREMENTS

■ Organizations must have documented procedures for the identification, collection, indexing, access, filing, storage, maintenance, and disposition of records.

■ Records must be maintained to demonstrate conformance to requirements and the effective operation of the quality system.

■ Pertinent subcontractor records must be included.

■ Records must be legible and stored and retained so they are readily retrievable.

■ A suitable environment must be provided to prevent damage, deterioration, and loss.

■ Record retention times must be established and recorded.

■ When contractually agreed upon, records must be available for evaluation by the customer or representative for an agreed period.

WHAT'S NEW

4 Quality management system
Clarifications

■ ISO 9001:2000 explicitly requires that records be controlled. *(Reference 4.2.3 Control of documents)*

■ The word "quality" has been removed in conjunction with records. *(Reference 4.2.4 Control of records)*

New Requirements

■ None

5 Management responsibility
Clarifications

■ None

New Requirements

■ None

4.16 CONTROL OF QUALITY RECORDS

6 Resource management
Clarifications
■ None

New Requirements
■ The requirement for organizations to keep training records has been broadened to include records of education, experience, training, and skills. *(Reference 6.2.2 Competence, awareness, and training)*

7 Product realization
Clarifications
■ Organizations must ensure that records provide evidence that the processes and resulting product meet requirements. *(Reference 7.1 Planning of product realization)*

New Requirements
■ The following records were included in ISO 9001:1994; however, the requirement to record results and necessary actions has been added:
  • Records for contract review must be more explicit. Rather than having a general record requirement, ISO 9001:2000 specifies that the results of the review and resultant actions must be recorded. *(Reference 7.2.2 Review of requirements related to the product)*
  • Reviews at suitable stages of design and development must be conducted. The results of the design and development reviews and necessary actions must be recorded and maintained. *(Reference 7.3.4 Design and development review)*
  • The results of verification and necessary actions must be recorded and maintained. *(Reference 7.3.5 Design and development verification)*
  • The results of validation and necessary actions must be recorded and maintained. *(Reference 7.3.6 Design and development validation)*
  • The results of the review of changes and necessary actions must be recorded and maintained. *(Reference 7.3.7 Control of design and development changes)*

4.16 CONTROL OF QUALITY RECORDS

- The results of supplier evaluations and necessary actions must be recorded and maintained. *(Reference 7.4.1 Purchasing process)*
- The results of calibration and verification must be recorded and maintained. *(Reference 7.6 Control of monitoring and measuring devices)*

8 Measurement, analysis, and improvement
Clarifications
■ None

New Requirements
■ Records must be kept for preventive action. *(Reference 8.5.3 Preventive action)*

What's the Same
■ Organizations must have a documented procedure that explains their record-keeping system.
■ The following records are still required in ISO 9001:2000:
- Management reviews *(Reference 5.6.1 General)*
- Training *(Reference 6.2.2 Competence, awareness, and training)*
- Contract review *(Reference 7.2.2 Review of requirements related to the product)*
- Supplier evaluations *(Reference 7.4.1 Purchasing process)*
- The unique identification of products where traceability is a requirement *(Reference 7.5.3 Identification and traceability)*
- Customer property that is lost, damaged, or unsuitable for use *(Reference 7.5.4 Customer property)*
- Qualified processes *(Reference 7.5.2 Validation of processes for production and service provision)*
- Calibration records for inspection, measuring, and test equipment. *(Reference 7.6 Control of monitoring and measuring devices)*
- Where no standards exist, the basis used for calibration *(Reference 7.6 Control of monitoring and measuring devices)*
- Results of internal audits *(Reference 8.2.2 Internal audit)*

4.16 CONTROL OF QUALITY RECORDS

- Implied records for follow-up activities that verify corrective action implementation *(Reference 8.2.2 Internal audit)*
- Inspection records authorizing the release of product *(Reference 8.2.4 Monitoring and measurement of product)*
- Results of corrective actions *(Reference 8.5.2 Corrective action)*

WHAT'S NOT INCLUDED

■ The requirement for collection, indexing, access, and filing has been removed.

■ The requirement for records of nonconformities accepted by the customer is no longer stated.

■ The specific reference to subcontractor records in 4.16 has been removed.

■ The legibility requirement of records has been removed but is implied in 4.2.3 Control of documents.

■ The requirement for a suitable environment to prevent damage, deterioration, and prevention of loss has been removed.

■ The requirement for making records available to the customer under contract is no longer stated.

■ The note that reminds the user that records can be any type of media has been removed, but it's implied in a note in 4.2.1 General.

IN A NUTSHELL

Many of the previous record requirements have stayed in place. However, subtle wording changes imply that more than just the evidence of a record will be required. For instance, under both customer information and design, results of the review and necessary actions will need to be recorded. In the past, most organizations could show that the record existed. ISO 9001:2000 requires auditors to look more closely at the results and actions of the activities instead of just at the paperwork. Finally, the word "quality" is no longer used in conjunction with records.

4.17 INTERNAL QUALITY AUDITS

1994 REQUIREMENTS
■ Organizations must have documented procedures for planning and implementing internal quality audits.
■ Internal audits must be scheduled.
■ Internal audits must be carried out by independent personnel.
■ Internal audit results must be recorded.
■ Those responsible for the areas being audited must be informed of the audit results.
■ Management must take timely corrective action on problems found during the audit.
■ Follow-up activities must verify and record that the corrective actions taken are implemented and effective.

WHAT'S NEW

5 Management responsibility
Clarifications
■ The standard more explicitly states that internal audit results must be a part of the management reviews. Management reviews must include information relating to the internal audit results. This requirement appeared in the note under internal audits in ISO 9001:1994. *(Reference 5.6.2 Review input)*

New Requirements
■ None

6 Resource management
Clarifications
■ None

New Requirements
■ None

4.17 INTERNAL QUALITY AUDITS

7 Product realization
Clarifications
■ None

New Requirements
■ None

8 Measurement, analysis, and improvement
Clarifications
■ ISO 9001:2000 clarifies the following:
  • The purpose of internal audits is to determine whether the quality management system conforms to the standard and the QMS requirements established by the organization and if the system has been effectively implemented and maintained.
  • The audit program must also be based on previous audit results.
  • The selection and conduct of the auditors is objective and impartial. Auditors can't audit their own work.
  • The audit procedure must define the responsibilities and requirements for planning and conducting audits, reporting results, and maintaining records.
  • Audit criteria, the audit scope, audit frequency, and methods used must be defined.
  (Reference 8.2.2 Internal audit)

New Requirements
■ Audit results must be used to continually improve the effectiveness of the QMS. *(Reference 8.5.1 Continual improvement)*

WHAT'S THE SAME
■ Organizations must have documented procedures for planning and implementing internal audits.
■ Internal audits must be scheduled, carried out by independent personnel, and the results must be recorded.
■ Those responsible for the areas being audited must be informed of the audit results (implied).

4.17 INTERNAL QUALITY AUDITS

■ Management must take timely corrective action on problems found during audits.
■ Follow-up audit activities must verify actions taken and be reported.

WHAT'S NOT INCLUDED
■ None

IN A NUTSHELL

All of the requirements have been carried over from ISO 9001:1994. The revision requires organizations to review their internal audit procedures to ensure the inclusion of responsibilities, requirements, and methodologies for conducting the audits. Audit results are now an explicit requirement for management review and for the facilitation of continual improvement activities.

The auditing techniques that internal auditors use may change slightly. Namely, auditors will need to determine a methodology of systems auditing that takes a cross-functional, process-oriented approach to developing checklists, conducting audits, and reporting the results. It's recommended that internal auditors receive additional training, as appropriate, on new auditing techniques for ISO 9001:2000.

4.18 TRAINING

1994 REQUIREMENTS

■ Organizations must have documented procedures for identifying training needs and providing training to those who perform activities affecting quality.

■ Personnel performing assigned work must be qualified.

■ Records of the training must be maintained.

WHAT'S NEW

5 Management responsibility
Clarifications
■ None

New Requirements
■ None

6 Resource management
Clarifications
■ Those performing work affecting quality must be competent based on their education, training, skills, and experience. *(Reference 6.2.1 General)*

New Requirements
■ The organization must determine necessary competence and provide training or other actions to satisfy competency needs. *(Reference 6.2.2 Competence, awareness, and training)*
■ The requirement for organizations to keep training records has been expanded to include records of education, experience, training, and skills. *(Reference 6.2.2 Competence, awareness, and training)*
■ Employees must understand the relevance and importance of what they do and how they contribute to the achievement of the quality objectives. *(Reference 6.2.2 Competence, awareness, and training)*
■ Organizations must evaluate the effectiveness of the training or actions they provide. *(Reference 6.2.2 Competence, awareness, and training)*

4.18 TRAINING

7 Product realization
Clarifications
- None

New Requirements
- None

8 Measurement, analysis, and improvement
Clarifications
- None

New Requirements
- None

WHAT'S THE SAME
- Organizations must:
  - Determine training needs
  - Provide training to meet these needs
  - Maintain records of training
  - Qualify their personnel

WHAT'S NOT INCLUDED
- A documented procedure for training is no longer specified.

IN A NUTSHELL
In addition to addressing training needs and qualifications of personnel, organizations must now describe how they will determine the effectiveness of their training and the competency of their people. A gray area of this section is the difference between competence and qualification. Although "competence" and "qualification" are synonyms, many would agree that individuals can be qualified but may not necessarily be competent to carry out the job. Consequently, organizations should consider defining what competency means to them

4.18 TRAINING

and how they would demonstrate this within their quality management system. Organizations must also ensure that their employees are aware of the importance of their activities and how they, as individuals, contribute to achieving the quality objectives. Also, ISO 9001:2000 now specifies what types of training records must be kept *(see Chapter 5, Transition Planning, for further clarification on training)*.

4.19 SERVICING

1994 REQUIREMENTS
■ Organizations must have documented procedures for performing, verifying, and reporting that servicing meets specified conditions when servicing is a requirement.

WHAT'S NEW

5 Management responsibility
Clarifications
■ None

New Requirements
■ None

6 Resource management
Clarifications
■ None

New Requirements
■ None

7 Product realization
Clarifications
■ Organizations must implement and carry out post-delivery activities under controlled conditions as applicable. *(Reference 7.5.1 Control of production and service provision)*

New Requirements
■ None

8 Measurement, analysis, and improvement
Clarifications
■ None

4.19 SERVICING

New Requirements
■ None

WHAT'S THE SAME
■ See "In a Nutshell."

WHAT'S NOT INCLUDED
■ See "In a Nutshell."

IN A NUTSHELL

ISO 9001:1994's requirements for servicing as it relates to repairs, maintenance, or other services specified in the original contract, and which is to take place after delivery, are blended into section 7.5.1, Control of production and service provision. ISO 9001:2000 no longer specifically addresses the need for documented procedures when performing, verifying, and reporting the servicing aspect, as was interpreted from ISO 9001:1994.

4.20 STATISTICAL TECHNIQUES

1994 REQUIREMENTS

■ Organizations must identify the statistical techniques necessary to establish, control, and verify process capability and product characteristics.

■ Organizations must have documented procedures for the implementation and use of the statistical techniques identified.

WHAT'S NEW

4 Quality management system
Clarifications
■ None

New Requirements
■ Organizations must monitor, measure, and analyze the processes they establish and implement actions to achieve planned results and continual improvement of the processes. *(Reference 4.1 General requirements)*

5 Management responsibility
Clarifications
■ None

New Requirements
■ None

6 Resource management
Clarifications
■ None

New Requirements
■ None

4.20 STATISTICAL TECHNIQUES

7 Product realization
Clarifications
■ None

New Requirements
■ None

8 Measurement, analysis, and improvement
Clarifications
■ Organizations must define, plan, and implement methods for measuring and monitoring activities. These activities must ensure that requirements are met and that the effectiveness of the quality management system is continually improved. ISO 9001:2000 makes it clear that measurements must be used and are not an option. *(Reference 8.1 General)*

New Requirements
■ Monitoring customer perceptions must be one of the measures of an organization's quality management system performance. *(Reference 8.2.1 Customer satisfaction)*
■ The methods for obtaining and using customer information must be defined. *(Reference 8.2.1 Customer satisfaction)*
■ Organizations must apply methods for measuring and monitoring processes to achieve planned results. *(Reference 8.2.3 Monitoring and measurement of processes)*
■ Product characteristics must be measured and monitored to verify that product requirements are met. *(Reference 8.2.4 Monitoring and measurement of product)*
■ Organizations must determine, collect, and analyze data to demonstrate the suitability/effectiveness of the system and to evaluate where continual improvement of the effectiveness of the QMS can be made. Data generated from monitoring and measuring activities must be included. *(Reference 8.4 Analysis of data)*
■ Analysis of data must provide information relating to customer satisfaction, conformity to product requirements, and characteristics and trends of processes, products, and suppliers. *(Reference 8.4 Analysis of data).*

4.20 STATISTICAL TECHNIQUES

■ Organizations must facilitate improvement activities through the analysis of data. *(Reference 8.5.1 Continual improvement)*

WHAT'S THE SAME
■ Organizations must determine the need for and application of methods, including statistical techniques.

WHAT'S NOT INCLUDED
■ A documented procedure to implement and control the application of statistical techniques is no longer specified.

IN A NUTSHELL
ISO 9001:2000 specifically requires the use of analysis and measurements to facilitate improvement activities. The 1994 version suggested that an organization first identify the need for statistical techniques, and if such a need wasn't found, the requirements didn't apply. It's apparent that measurements will need to be implemented and used to achieve conformity and for improvement activities. ISO 9001:2000 makes it clear that monitoring customer perceptions is one of the measurements of performance.

For many organizations, implementation of this section will be a challenge. The maturity of an organization's measurement systems will determine the amount of effort and development needed. In other words, if organizations have measurements in place, they will need to evaluate those measurements and the results they will provide. The main point to remember is that ISO 9001:2000 focuses on using measurements and their results to drive continual improvement.

Chapter 4

Noteworthy Changes

A lthough ISO 9001:2000's new requirements were specifically identified in Chapter 3, Comparing ISO 9001:1994 with ISO 9001:2000, this chapter further explains some of the new requirements to provide additional understanding. Organizations will need to thoroughly comprehend the impact of these requirements and determine what actions are necessary to comply with ISO 9001:2000. Keep in mind that some organizations may not currently have a system in place to address these requirements.

PROCESS MODEL STRUCTURE

The most radical change in ISO 9001:2000 is the elimination of the 4.1–4.20 clause format. By using tools such as the cross-reference matrix found in this book and understanding the process approach, organizations already familiar with ISO 9001:1994 will be able to make the necessary changes. Though the original purpose of the 1994 version may not have changed, ISO 9001:2000 requires careful reading as many of the terms and requirements have been modified or reworded.

MANAGEMENT AND CONTINUAL IMPROVEMENT

One of the key changes in ISO 9001:2000 requires management to use the information from the quality management system to implement improvements. The initial requirements begin under section 5.3 Quality policy, in which the standard requires management to show a commitment to quality by meeting the requirements and continually improving the effectiveness of the quality management system. This is further emphasized in section 8.4 Analysis of data, which requires organizations to collect and analyze data to determine the effectiveness of their quality management system and to identify improvements. Finally, in section 8.5.1 Continual improvement, organizations are required to continually improve the effectiveness of the quality management system through the use of the following:

■ Quality policy
■ Quality objectives
■ Audit results
■ Analysis of data
■ Corrective and preventive actions
■ Management review

Although some organizations use information effectively, many organizations don't use the information from their quality management system to initiate improvement activities. These requirements may prove to be a challenge for such organizations.

5.4.2 QUALITY MANAGEMENT SYSTEM PLANNING

Organizations should carefully review their quality management system planning activities. ISO 9001:2000 section 5.4.2 Quality management system planning requires that quality objectives be aligned with planning activities. Section 7.1 Planning of product realization links quality objectives and the requirements needed to make a product. Section 5.4.2 Quality management system planning also requires management to pay attention to changes that may occur in the organization such as implementation of computer systems, changes in management representatives, downsizing, and so on to ensure that the integrity of the quality management system remains intact during these changes.

THE VOICE OF THE CUSTOMER

One of the fundamental differences between the ISO 9001:1994 and ISO 9001:2000 is the new requirements that are specifically focused on the organization's customers. One of the criticisms of ISO 9001:1994 was that it focused on the organization and its suppliers rather than on the customer. ISO 9001:2000 includes several sections that focus directly on the customer. Following is a brief description of each:

5.2 CUSTOMER FOCUS

Although this section is short, it has a powerful message: It is the responsibility of top management to ensure that their customers' requirements are determined and met in order to enhance customer satisfaction.

Unfortunately, organizations don't always make what their customers want. Instead, they make what they think their customers want. Section 5.2 Customer focus specifically directs organizations toward a formal mechanism to ensure customer satisfaction through measurements of performance. For some organizations, this may be a new concept, or at least one that has not been effectively implemented.

7.2 CUSTOMER-RELATED PROCESSES

This section is broken up into three subsections. Two of the three sections are new. Each section deals with a different aspect of customer interaction and is listed below:

■ 7.2.1 Determination of requirements related to the product focuses specifically on the type of customer requirements that must be determined:
- customer-specific product requirements, including delivery and post-delivery activities
- product requirements not stated by the customer but necessary for specified or intended use where known
- regulatory and statutory requirements
- additional requirements decided by the organization

■ 7.2.2 Review of requirements related to product is basically the same as ISO 9001:1994's 4.3 Contract Review clause. Organizations must understand their customers' requirements and have the ability to meet the requirements prior to accepting the order.

■ 7.2.3 Customer communication requires organizations to determine and implement communication "arrangements" (methods) with their customers. Many organizations probably do this already, but they may not have their process formalized. The information exchanged between the organization and its customers is related to products, inquiries, contracts, order handling, changes, complaints, and feedback.

8.2.1 CUSTOMER SATISFACTION

The ease with which organizations are able to comply with this requirement will depend on the maturity of the organizations and their relationships with their customers. It will also depend on whether the organizations have a customer satisfaction measurement system in place and how effective it is. The requirement states that organizations must monitor information relating to customer perception regarding meeting customer requirements as a performance measurement of their quality management systems. Furthermore, organizations must determine the methodologies for obtaining and using this information. The intent of this requirement is to ensure that organizations have a customer complaint and general feedback system in place, and that it is effective for addressing customer concerns.

INTERNAL COMMUNICATION

5.5.3 Internal communication requires organizations to focus on how they communicate information throughout their various levels and functions. Specifically, the requirement is concerned with the communication of information that pertains to the effectiveness of the quality management system. Many organizations may have a formal communication mechanism at the top and middle management levels. However, this new requirement clearly emphasizes top management's responsibility to ensure the establishment of appropriate communication processes. In ISO 9001:1994, only the quality policy had to be communicated to all levels. Therefore, many organizations may need to consider how they share quality management system information within their workplace.

THE ORGANIZATION
6.1 PROVISION OF RESOURCES

The focus of this section is very clear: Organizations must provide needed resources to enhance customer satisfaction and implement, maintain, and improve the effectiveness of their quality management system. It will be up to the organizations to determine whether additional resources will be necessary to meet this requirement. This requirement is tied to management review, which now specifically states that the outputs from the review must include actions relating to resource needs.

6.3 INFRASTRUCTURE

This section contains one of ISO 9001:2000's biggest gray areas. It requires organizations to be responsible for identifying, providing, and maintaining the infrastructure needed to make good products. This section includes three areas:

- Workspace and associated utilities—this implies the inclusion of the employees' work area and the building itself
- Equipment, hardware, and software—basically from ISO 9001:1994's 4.9 Process Control
- Supporting services—implies inclusion of the preventive maintenance activities as well as transportation or communication.

The ISO 9004:2000 guideline should be reviewed for more insight into defining the infrastructure requirement.

6.4 WORK ENVIRONMENT

This section indicates that organizations are responsible for determining and managing the work environment needed to achieve good products. When managing the work environment, factors that should be considered include safety rules, ergonomics, humidity, heat, noise, and cleanliness. ISO 9004:2000 provides further description of these factors.

DOCUMENTATION REQUIREMENTS

An important change in the procedural requirements for the ISO 9001:2000 standard is the fact that the number of specifically required documented procedures has been changed as follows:

- 4.2.3   Control of documents
- 4.2.4   Control of records
- 8.2.2   Internal audit
- 8.3   Control of nonconforming product
- 8.5.2   Corrective action
- 8.5.3   Preventive action

While the number of required documented procedures has been reduced, it does not mean that organizations will be able to forgo documentation or its control. In the standard, under Section 4, Quality management system, more responsibility is placed on the organization to decide which documents it will need to ensure the effective planning, operation, and control of its processes. Section 4 also requires that the organization identify the processes needed for the quality management system and the application of these processes as well as their sequence and interaction. The documentation system must also include documented statements of a quality policy, quality objectives, a quality manual, and records as required by the standard.

When determining the amount of documentation needed, the organization should base its decision on the size of the organization, the complexity of its activities and processes as well as the competence of its personnel. It should also be noted that the documentation may be any type of medium, including hard copy or electronic versions. With many organizations moving toward electronic methods, controls must be established and implemented.

IN A NUTSHELL

Many of the new requirements are designed to ensure that top management is involved in the quality management system. This includes clearly understanding their customers' requirements and converting these requirements into quality products that ensure customer satisfaction. Furthermore, ISO 9001:2000 specifies that a process must exist for determining these customer requirements and that top management is to ensure that all personnel understand the importance of meeting customer requirements.

Organizations are now responsible for determining and implementing a communication mechanism with their customers as it pertains to inquiries, orders, and complaints of product and/or service. ISO 9001:2000 expands upon ISO 9001:1994's 4.3 Contract Review clause by ensuring that organizations are delivering the product and/or service their customers want. Furthermore, top management must ensure that people at all levels communicate information relating to the effectiveness of the quality management system.

Managers must also be specific in their intent when aligning the quality policy, objectives, and commitment with planning and continual improvement activities. They must ensure that the needed resources are provided in a timely manner to implement and improve processes and to enhance customer satisfaction.

Finally, with the changes in the documentation requirements, organizations will still need to demonstrate control of their quality management system to both internal and external auditors. This will apply to both the documentation required by the standard as well as the documentation determined by the organization.

Chapter 5

Transition Planning

A smooth transition to ISO 9001:2000 will require careful consideration of documentation, training, auditing, and management. Each of these is described in this chapter, along with some transition "tips." The length of time it takes an organization to successfully become compliant to ISO 9001:2000 will depend on the maturity of its quality management system, the level of management's commitment, the number of adequately assigned resources, and the solidity of its action plan.

DOCUMENTATION

One of the first questions organizations face in the transition from ISO 9001:1994 to ISO 9001:2000 is whether they will need to change their documentation structure. The answer is a resounding "no!" Organizations aren't required to change the structure (i.e., levels or tiers) or the numbering schemes of their documentation. They will, however, need to incorporate the new requirements into their current quality management system. It's essential that organizations be able to show internal and third-party auditors how the integration of ISO 9001:2000 requirements is documented.

Organizations will be able to note "exclusions" as appropriate for their situations. Organizations may only exclude requirements within section 7, Product realization, that are related to the nature of the organization's product, the customer requirements, and the applicable regulatory requirements.

As was discussed earlier in Chapter 4, ISO 9001:2000 reduces the requirements for documented procedures. However, it states that organizations must plan their processes for product realization and must determine the need for these processes and documentation. Even though this is the case, organizations should not "undocument" any parts of their existing quality management system. In fact, they are encouraged to maintain this documentation as objective evidence of their system.

Organizations should also pay close attention to the implications of ISO 9001:2000's section 4, Quality management system, which stipulates that organizations must document their quality management system. In addition, 4.1 requires organizations to identify processes and determine the sequence and interaction of these processes. To provide evidence that these tasks have been accomplished, documentation is necessary.

Section 4.2.1 General, within the documentation requirements, mandates that organizations include their own documentation in their quality management system to ensure effective operation and control of processes. The extent of documentation depends on the size and type of the organization, complexity and interaction of processes, and the competence of personnel. ISO 9001:2000 gives a great deal of latitude surrounding documentation, but competence of personnel may be a key factor when determining the amount of documentation needed. For example, if employees cannot demonstrate knowledge or if inconsistent practices between employees are identified and few documented procedures exist, internal or external auditors may conclude that the processes or systems are incomplete or that training isn't effective. Organizations will need to challenge the lack of documentation as well as the overabundance of documentation.

As a reminder, documentation can be in electronic form or on paper. As many organizations move toward electronic procedures and record keeping, they will need to apply access control as well as establish effective back-up systems.

TIPS

■ Do a quick review of your current quality manual to ensure that it's ISO 9001:1994-compliant. Existing noncompliances with ISO 9001:1994 may cause problems as your organization tries to determine what changes need to be made.

■ Refer to the matrix in this book to help you make the correct links and cross-references to ISO 9001:2000 *(see page 107).*

■ Review all of the new requirements as stated in this book and in ISO 9001:2000 and determine which documentation actions, if any, are needed to become compliant.

■ Make sure that your quality manual is compliant to ISO 9001:2000 and is controlled. Keep in mind that if your organization plans to maintain its current documentation structure, the quality manual will be essential as a springboard to the rest of the documentation.

■ Develop a cross-reference matrix that shows how your organization's current documentation aligns with ISO 9001:2000 so that any existing gaps can be determined.

■ If you plan to use your organization's existing documentation numbering scheme, be sure to incorporate any new documents into that scheme.

■ If you plan to make changes to the structure of your organization's documentation for ease of understanding the standard, a logical modification would be to redesign the quality manual documentation to meet the new ISO 9001:2000 numbering scheme and make a cross-reference to existing documentation.

■ Retrain employees, as applicable, on documentation changes, and record the training.

TRAINING

In section 6.2.2 Competence, awareness, and training, two new concepts emerge. First, organizations must ensure that their employees are "aware" of how their activities contribute to the achievement of quality objectives. Second, personnel must be "competent" rather than just "trained." Some might argue that these terms are essentially the same; others would say that competence implies something beyond training: Competent people can demonstrate through their actions that they have been trained successfully. Keep in mind that the competency of personnel should be one of the main criteria for management to consider when determining the amount of documentation needed.

With today's rapidly changing business environment, organizations must continually determine the employee training needed to provide their customers with quality products and services that meet or exceed expectations. Because customers continue to want and expect more, organizations must periodically analyze their training and competency needs. After this analysis, organizations can compare identified needs against their current performances and document the gaps.

To close the training and competency gaps, organizations first need to define their competency needs. Once these are clear, organizations can design, plan, and provide the training. After the training has been conducted, organizations should have a mechanism in place to evaluate the outcome of the training to determine effectiveness.

■ Consider publicizing your organization's quality objectives in a format all employees can understand. Identify training objectives that will help the organization meet quality objectives.

■ Create a flowchart to show links between organizational activities and quality objectives that will clearly convey their importance and interaction.

■ Offer employees incentives based on the achievement of quality goals.

■ Make sure that your organization has accurately defined roles and responsibilities. Then define the competencies needed for quality-related tasks that match the roles and responsibilities, assess the personnel to perform the task, and develop plans to close the competency gaps.

■ Periodically re-evaluate the competency needs of personnel, particularly when business conditions cause change within the organization, and determine if any additional training is required.

■ Ensure that an evaluation system, based on established criteria, exists to verify that the required competence levels have been achieved.

■ Ensure that employees are trained on changes to the quality management system that affect their positions or departments. Include training for documentation or system revisions, and record the training.

■ Select trainers (external, on-the-job, or companywide) carefully and verify that they understand the importance of delivering training that can demonstrate a measurable outcome.

■ Ensure that training provided is evaluated for effectiveness.

AUDITING

Although the internal auditing requirements haven't changed in ISO 9001:2000, auditors will be required to have training in several additional areas. Because the process management approach is the fundamental concept for the application of ISO 9001:2000, auditors will need to be familiar with process management concepts and terminology found in ISO 9000:2000. For further guidance, refer to the terminology found in ISO 19011, a guideline for auditing, which is under revision and will cancel and replace ISO 10011.

Auditors are also required to have specific competencies in the eight quality management principles and techniques to enable them to examine the system to determine whether the application of requirements has been properly carried out. Organizations will need to assess how they are organized and determine what changes will need to be made in order to conduct their audits.

Auditors may experience difficulties because some of the requirements are no longer contained within a single clause or element as was the case in ISO 9001:1994. Auditors will need to understand how the revised requirements are structured if they are to complete a successful audit. For example, in ISO 9001:1994's section 4.10 Inspection and Testing, the requirements were contained within one clause. Now auditors will need to consider the requirements found in 7.4.3 Verification of purchased product for the receiving inspection, 8.2.4 Monitoring and measurement of product for the in-process and final inspection, and 7.5.3 Identification and traceability for inspection status requirements to thoroughly conduct the audit *(see Appendix 2)*.

The majority of the records required by ISO 9001:2000 must show results and necessary actions. As such, auditors will need to do more than check to see if a record exists. They will need to pay closer attention to documented results and any actions that were taken.

Some requirements fall into gray areas. One of the most challenging debates about ISO 9001:2000 centers on whether all requirements are specific enough to be auditable. Because the requirements for documented procedures have been changed, it will take a skilled auditor time and dedication to determine whether a department or organization has adequately defined its quality management system.

When planning and scheduling audits, organizations will need to take into consideration how requirements are aligned so that the requirements are audited logically. This means that organizations that used to set aside one week a year to conduct all of their required audits may need to rethink their strategy to conduct a thorough audit. Organizations may also find that they will need to initially plan audits with smaller scopes to allow their auditors to gain familiarity with ISO 9001:2000.

TIPS

■ Ensure that your internal auditors are familiar with the eight quality management principles upon which ISO 9001:2000 is based. *(See the section under "Management" for an explanation of the eight quality management principles.)*

■ Review audit checklists and determine which questions and approaches need to be modified to reflect ISO 9001:2000's process approach as well as to ensure that the new requirements are covered.

■ Review the audit plan and schedule to ensure that requirements are grouped together logically.

■ Take into consideration the scope of the audit. Smaller audits may allow the auditors to adjust to the revisions of the standard.
■ Ensure that the internal auditors are competent in systems auditing and understand how the system is linked.
■ Review and become familiar with the definitions and terminologies in *ISO 9000:2000 Quality management system—Fundamentals and vocabulary*.
■ Provide training for auditors on the revisions.

MANAGEMENT

ISO 9001:2000 removes responsibility for the quality management system from quality assurance. It requires top management to ensure that:
■ Customer requirements are fully understood and met in order to enhance customer satisfaction.
■ Planning activities include objectives at relevant functions and levels within the organization.
■ Internal communications are established.
■ Information within the system (e.g., data, internal audit results, customer measures) is used to facilitate improvement.

ISO 9001:2000 purposely directs top management to expand their role in the quality management system. ISO 9001:2000 addresses the organization as a whole, but top management's involvement will be necessary to determine the methods and policies surrounding many of the quality management system's requirements.

Management will also need to take an active role in reviewing current performance and improvement opportunities relating to changing circumstances within organizations, process and product conformance analysis, and customer satisfaction. Top management has the ultimate responsibility of ensuring that adequate resources are provided throughout the organization to implement, maintain, and continually improve the effectiveness of the quality management system and to enhance customer satisfaction.

EIGHT QUALITY MANAGEMENT PRINCIPLES

The eight quality management principles are focused on business excellence and place an emphasis on customer satisfaction. A quality management principle is a fundamental belief that is focused on the continual performance improvement of an organization through addressing the needs of customers and stakeholders. The principles are as follows:

1. *Customer Focus*—Organizations consider customers' current and future needs, fulfill customer requirements, and strive to exceed customer expectations.

2. *Leadership*—Leaders establish the organization's purpose and direction and create an environment in which people can be involved in achieving organizational objectives.

3. *Involvement of People*—An organization's people are its essence, and their involvement and abilities benefit the organization.

4. *Process Approach*—A process approach to managing resources and activities will produce the desired results.

5. *System Approach to Management*—An organization's efficiency and effectiveness can be improved by identifying, understanding, and managing a system of interrelated processes.

6. *Continual Improvement*—An organization should have continual improvement as a permanent objective.

7. *Factual Approach to Decision Making*—Organizations should analyze data and information in order to make effective decisions.

8. *Mutually Beneficial Supplier Relationships*—Both the organization and its suppliers can create value by developing mutually beneficial, interdependent relationships.

TIPS

Top management should:

■ Understand how customer needs and expectations are identified, converted into products and/or services, and communicated within the organization.

■ Ensure that a system is in place to measure customer satisfaction as well as to ensure that actions are taken on the results.

■ Ascertain how customer relationships are managed and initiate improvement actions for any identified gaps.

■ Ensure that organizational objectives are linked to customer needs and expectations.

■ Create an organizational vision and translate this vision into measurable goals and objectives.

■ Empower and involve people within the organization to achieve organizational objectives.

■ Utilize the process approach for operations as well as establish responsibility and authority for managing processes.

■ Align individual process goals and the organization's key objectives.

■ Determine the links between the organization's quality policy, quality objectives, audit results, data analysis, corrective and preventive actions, and management review, and determine how these links form the foundation for continual improvement.

■ Evaluate how well the organization utilizes measurements and data analysis as a basis for improvement of the quality management system.

■ Utilize the information from data analysis to assess process and system performance in order to facilitate continual improvement.

■ Evaluate the relationships with suppliers and identify areas for improvement that will be mutually beneficial.

IN A NUTSHELL

Accreditation bodies around the world have decided that ISO 9001:1994, ISO 9002:1994, and ISO 9003:1994 will be valid for three years after the official ISO release date of ISO 9001:2000, which was December 15, 2000. This decision allows time for ISO 9001:2000 to be translated into native languages. Also, due to the nature of the revisions, it's expected that organizations registered to ISO 9001, ISO 9002 or ISO 9003 will need time to make the transition to ISO 9001:2000. Although organizations that are currently registered have up to three years to make the transition, they are encouraged to make the transition as soon as possible. ISO recommends that certification/registration bodies urge their clients to make the transition to ISO 9001:2000 before their registration to the 1994 version expires. It will be the organization's responsibility to be in close contact with its registrar about specific timing requirements that the registrar may impose.

Chapter 6

Answers to Common Concerns

T his chapter provides answers to some of the most frequently asked questions about ISO 9001:2000. The chapter is divided into seven question categories:
1. Purpose and Benefits
2. Modifications to the ISO 9000 Standards Family
3. Releasing the Revisions
4. Registration Concerns
5. Auditing Issues
6. Service and Small Organizations
7. Other Information

1. PURPOSE AND BENEFITS

What is the purpose of revising the ISO 9000 standards?

ISO has issued directives that require standards to be revised on a periodic basis so that the needs of the global business community are satisfied. User surveys have found that companies are looking for closer alignment of their quality management system with the way they actually run their businesses. ISO 9001:2000 is intended to emphasize the measurement of customer satisfaction, process management utilization, and information analysis to drive continuous improvement.

What is the focus of ISO 9001:2000, and why does this benefit my organization?

Some of the most significant points of the revised standard include its emphasis on using a process-related structure, using information from the system to facilitate improvement, and including customer satisfaction in improvement activities.

Many of the criticisms of the previous versions of the ISO 9000 series focused on disconnected processes and the lack of emphasis on improvement activities. ISO 9001:2000 stresses the importance of tying information from customer satisfaction measures, audit results, corrective/ preventive action results, and other measures to management activities in order to facilitate improvement.

ISO 9001:2000 has also attempted to address the needs and interests of organizations and specific sectors (such as telecommunication, automotive, etc.) and was designed to be compatible with other management systems, such as ISO 14001:1996.

How are financial issues addressed in ISO 9001:2000?

Financial issues are not addressed in ISO 9001:2000. However, ISO 9004:2000 does include considerations for satisfying the needs and expectations of owners and investors.

I've heard that showing evidence of improvement is now a requirement. What will I be required to do to achieve this?

One of ISO 9001:2000's focuses is to ensure that information collected from the quality management system is used for the purpose of implementing improvement. Organizations can best meet this requirement by ensuring that information such as audit results, customer satisfaction/ dissatisfaction reports, and corrective/preventive action results are reviewed by management and that appropriate actions are taken. In the past, many organizations collected this information but didn't take action, such as comparing trends or looking at all information collectively, to determine where improvements could be made.

2. MODIFICATIONS TO THE ISO 9000 STANDARDS FAMILY

I've heard that there will no longer be an ISO 9002 or an ISO 9003 standard. Why?

The requirements of both of these standards are included in ISO 9001:2000. You will be able to tailor the standard according to your organization's activities. For example, if your organization is currently registered to ISO 9002:1994, your revised ISO 9001:2000 quality system manual would be changed from the statement that 4.4 Design Control doesn't apply and be replaced with the statement that 7.3 Design and development does not apply to your organization.

There are other documents within the ISO 9000 family. What will happen to them?

With more than 20 standards and documents in the ISO 9000 family, there appears to be a proliferation of standards. This has been a concern of ISO 9000 users. Therefore, the revised ISO 9000 family will only consist of four core standards: ISO 9000 (formerly *ISO 8402 vocabulary*), ISO 9001, ISO 9004, and ISO 19011 *(Guidelines on quality and/or environmental management systems auditing)*. The ISO 9000 family also includes *ISO 10012 Measurement Control System*, which is not considered a core document. Subsequently, the other documents will become obsolete or be replaced by technical reports.

I've heard that ISO 9001:2000 and ISO 9004:2000 are a "consistent pair." What does this mean?

The term "consistent pair" refers to the ISO 9001:2000 and ISO 9004:2000 quality management standards. These two standards have been specifically designed to be compatible with one another. Although each standard may be used independently, the overall benefits to organizations may be more extensive if the two standards are fully implemented together. For ease of use, ISO 9004:2000 includes the requirements from ISO 9001:2000, which is a significant change from the 1994 version.

ISO 9001:2000 is used for registration purposes and it defines the minimum requirements needed to achieve customer satisfaction. Although ISO 9004:2000 may not be used for registration, it's recommended that managers who wish to move beyond the basic requirements of ISO 9001:2000 use ISO 9004:2000 as a guide in their pursuit of a more robust quality management system.

ISO 9004:2000 also contains a self-assessment tool to assist organizations in determining the maturity of their quality management system. It should also be noted that ISO 9004:2000 should not be used as a guidance document for compliance to ISO 9001:2000.

3. RELEASING THE REVISIONS

In which languages will ISO 9001:2000 be available?

ISO 9001:2000 will be published in three official languages: English, French, and Russian.

Because ISO 9001:2000 is now published, will my organization have to change our quality management system's documentation structure?

No. You will not have to change your structure; however, you will have to incorporate the new requirements into your quality management system in the relevant areas. Some organizations may choose to restructure their quality manuals to match the new numbering scheme. This decision will be up to the individual organization.

4. REGISTRATION CONCERNS

If my organization is currently registered to ISO 9002:1994, how will the revised standard affect our registration?

Accredited certificates issued to ISO 9001/9002/9003:1994 will expire on December 15, 2003. If you currently hold an ISO 9002 certificate, you can still explain the reduction of scope within your quality manual as previously done for such elements as 4.4 Design Control.

What if my organization chooses to keep our system compliant to the 1994 version? Will we be able to remain certified?

No. The 1994 version will be valid until December 15, 2003. This time frame is dependent on your registrar's requirements and, potentially, your surveillance audit schedule. After this established time frame, if your system is not updated, it will be considered noncompliant.

I work for an ISO 9002-registered company. How will we be able to tell the difference between companies with design responsibilities and those without design responsibilities now that the standard only reflects ISO 9001?

Organizations will require very clear and concise descriptions of their activities that are to be included in the registration process. Also, certification/registration bodies will need to take particular care in defining the scope of the certificates issued.

Will it be possible to register my organization's quality system to the ISO 9004:2000 document?

No. ISO 9004:2000 is a guidance document only and is not intended for certification purposes.

Because ISO 9001:2000 is now released, will a full reassessment of my organization be required?

This is primarily a decision to be made between your organization and your registrar. It will also depend upon how quickly an organization is able to upgrade its quality management system. Accreditation bodies worldwide will be providing guidance for the numerous certification bodies on how to proceed regarding this issue.

Will I need to rewrite all of my documentation to comply with the process model approach?

Every organization should carefully think through how it will approach the revisions. If the current documentation has been written well and is compliant, there should not be a need to rewrite all of the documentation. The organization will need to review the revisions against its current documentation in order to determine the changes needed.

5. AUDITING ISSUES

Will we need to retrain our internal auditors?

Yes. You will need to train your internal auditors on the structure, content, and terminology of the revised standard. The auditors will need to understand the process management concept and will need to develop auditing checklists that cover the processes within your organization as they relate to ISO 9001:2000's requirements. They should also be familiar with the eight quality management principles.

Will third-party auditors need to be retrained?

Yes. The third-party auditors received adequate training prior to the release of ISO 9001:2000.

Third-party auditors will need to audit your organization using a process-oriented approach. Rather than focusing on the ISO 9001 requirements within a particular function, they will focus on entire business processes across the organization. They will need to determine how those business processes and the associated documentation meet the ISO 9001:2000 requirements.

Has a common auditing standard for ISO 9001 and ISO 14001 been developed?

ISO 10011, the common guideline document for auditing, is being consolidated with ISO 14010, ISO 14011, and ISO 14012. This new document is titled *ISO 19011 Guidelines on quality and/or environmental management systems auditing.* Keep in mind that this is a guidance document providing a foundation for structuring the audit system.

6. SERVICE AND SMALL ORGANIZATIONS

Will small organizations still be able to adapt the requirements of the standard to fit their needs?

From the very beginning, one of the intents behind ISO 9001 was that the standard be generic enough to adapt to any organization, small or large, manufacturing or service. This intent has not changed. As in the past, it will be up to the individual organization to determine the level of complexity needed to meet its organizational and customer needs.

My organization provides services. Will the revised standard apply to us?

ISO 9001:2000 is intended to apply to all types of organizations, including those in the service industry. The standard is written in generic terms and is adaptable to small, medium, and large organizations.

7. OTHER INFORMATION

If I want to know more about the revised standards, where can I get the information?

There are a number of sources from which to get information:
■ American Society for Quality (ASQ)—(800) 248-1946 or *www.asq.org*
■ Registrar Accreditation Board (RAB)—(888) 722-2440 or *www.rabnet.com*
■ U.S. Standards Group—*standardsgroup.asq.org*

The standards can be ordered from ASQ. Information can also be obtained from ISO's Web site at *www.iso.ch.*

You may also contact the authors of this book:
Jeanne Ketola, CEO
Pathway Consulting Inc.
Minneapolis, Minnesota
www.pathwayconsultinginc.com

Kathy Roberts, President
Sunrise Consulting Inc.
Raleigh, North Carolina
http://thesunrise.home.mindspring.com

You may also visit the authors' joint Web site:
www.inanutshellproductions.com

Appendix 1

Record Requirements

The following chart shows the records required for ISO 9001:2000. Keep in mind that most records need to demonstrate results and any necessary actions taken. ISO 9001:2000 explicitly requires that records be controlled.

Organizations should also carefully review ISO 9001:2000 for required documentation that is not considered a record or a procedure. This includes items such as the quality policy, quality objectives, and the quality manual.

ISO 9001:2000 Records by Section

Section	Description
4.2.1 General	Reference to records required by the standard
4.2.3 Control of documents	Records are controlled according to 4.2.4
4.2.4 Control of records	Records are established and maintained to provide evidence of conformity
5.6.1 Management Review– General	Management review records
6.2.2 Competence, awareness, and training	Education, training, skills, and experience
7.1 Planning of product realization	Evidence is recorded that the realization processes and resulting product meet requirements
7.2.2 Review of requirements related to the product	Results of the review and actions arising from the review
7.3.2 Design and development inputs	Inputs relating to product requirements
7.3.4 Design and development review	Results of the reviews and any necessary actions
7.3.5 Design and development verification	Results of the verification and any necessary actions
7.3.6 Design and development validation	Records of the results of validation and any necessary actions

ISO 9001:2000 Records by Section

Section	Description
7.3.7 Control of design and development changes	Results of the review of changes and any necessary actions
7.4.1 Purchasing process	Results of supplier evaluations and any necessary actions arising from the evaluation
7.5.2 Validation of processes for production and service provision	Requirements for records as applicable
7.5.3 Identification and traceability	Where traceability is a requirement, the unique identification of the product
7.5.4 Customer property	Records of customer property that is lost, damaged, or unsuitable for use
7.6 Control of monitoring and measuring devices	• Where no standards exist, basis used for calibration is recorded • Records of the results of calibration and verification are maintained
8.2.2 Internal audit	• Records of audit results • Implied records for reporting verification follow-up activities and results
8.2.4 Monitoring and measurement of product	Record indicates the person(s) authorizing the release of the product
8.3 Control of nonconforming product	The nature of nonconformities and any subsequent actions taken, including concessions obtained
8.5.2 Corrective action	Records for corrective action results taken
8.5.3 Preventive action	Records for preventive action results taken

Appendix 2

Clause-to-Section Cross-Reference Matrix

The chart on the following pages compares ISO 9001:1994's clauses to ISO 9001:2000's sections. 1994's 20 clauses are shown across the top of the matrix. ISO 9001:2000's sections 4–8 are listed down the left side of the matrix.

ISO 9001:1994's 20 clauses are:

4.1	Management Responsibility
4.2	Quality System
4.3	Contract Review
4.4	Design Control
4.5	Document and Data Control
4.6	Purchasing
4.7	Control of Customer-Supplied Product
4.8	Product Identification and Traceability
4.9	Process Control
4.10	Inspection and Testing
4.11	Control of Inspection, Measuring, and Test Equipment
4.12	Inspection and Test Status
4.13	Control of Nonconforming Product
4.14	Corrective and Preventive Action
4.15	Handling, Storage, Packaging, Preservation, and Delivery
4.16	Control of Quality Records
4.17	Internal Quality Audits
4.18	Training
4.19	Servicing
4.20	Statistical Techniques

ISO 9001:1994 Clauses (Across) / ISO 9001:2000 Sections (Down)	4.1	4.2	4.3	4.4	4.5	4.6	4.7	4.8	4.9	4.10	4.11	4.12	4.13	4.14	4.15	4.16	4.17	4.18	4.19	4.20
4 Quality management system																				
4.1 General requirements		■																		
4.2 Documentation requirements (title only)		■																		
4.2.1 General																				
4.2.2 Quality manual					■															
4.2.3 Control of documents																■				
4.2.4 Control of records																				
5 Management responsibility																				
5.1 Management commitment		■																		
5.2 Customer focus			■																	
5.3 Quality policy	■																			
5.4 Planning (title only)																				
5.4.1 Quality objectives		■																		
5.4.2 Quality management system planning		■																		
5.5 Responsibility, authority, and communication (title only)																				
5.5.1 Responsibility and authority	■																			
5.5.2 Management representative	■																			
5.5.3 Internal communication																				
5.6 Management review (title only)																				
5.6.1 General	■																			
5.6.2 Review input													■			■				
5.6.3 Review output																				
6 Resource management																				
6.1 Provision of resources	■	■																		
6.2 Human resources (title only)																				
6.2.1 General																				
6.2.2 Competence, awareness, and training																		■		
6.3 Infrastructure									■											
6.4 Work environment																				

ISO 9001:1994 Clauses (Across) / ISO 9001:2000 Sections (Down)	4.1	4.2	4.3	4.4	4.5	4.6	4.7	4.8	4.9	4.10	4.11	4.12	4.13	4.14	4.15	4.16	4.17	4.18	4.19	4.20
7 Product realization																				
7.1 Planning of product realization	■	■							■	■										
7.2 Customer-related processes (title only)			■																	
7.2.1 Determination of requirements related to the product			■																	
7.2.2 Review of requirements related to the product			■																	
7.2.3 Customer communication														■						
7.3 Design and development (title only)				■																
7.3.1 Design and development planning				■																
7.3.2 Design and development inputs				■																
7.3.3 Design and development outputs				■																
7.3.4 Design and development review				■												■				
7.3.5 Design and development verification				■												■				
7.3.6 Design and development validation				■												■				
7.3.7 Control of design and development changes				■																
7.4 Purchasing (title only)						■														
7.4.1 Purchasing process						■														
7.4.2 Purchasing information						■														
7.4.3 Verification of purchased product										■										
7.5 Production and service provision (title only)									■						■				■	
7.5.1 Control of production and service provision									■						■				■	
7.5.2 Validation of process for production and service provision									■		■				■	■				
7.5.3 Identification and traceability								■				■				■				
7.5.4 Customer property							■													
7.5.5 Preservation of product															■					
7.6 Control of monitoring and measuring devices											■									
8 Measurement, analysis, and improvement																				
8.1 General										■										■
8.2 Monitoring and measurement (title only)																				■
8.2.1 Customer satisfaction																				
8.2.2 Internal audit																	■			
8.2.3 Monitoring and measurement of processes									■							■				■
8.2.4 Monitoring and measurement of product										■		■								
8.3 Control of nonconforming product													■							
8.4 Analysis of data														■		■				■
8.5 Improvement (title only)																				
8.5.1 Continual improvement	■																			
8.5.2 Corrective action														■						
8.5.3 Preventive action														■						

About the Authors

Jeanne Ketola, CEO of Pathway Consulting Inc., has more than 20 years of business experience in a diverse range of industries. She has a bachelor's degree in business management and is an ASQ Certified Quality Auditor, an RAB Quality Systems Auditor, and a trained management coach. Ketola is actively involved in the U.S. TAG to TC 176, which reviews and approves the ISO 9000 standards for the United States. She has participated at a national level in writing the auditing guidelines for ISO 9000-Q10011. Ketola is the secretary of the ANSI Z1 Executive Committee, which is responsible for all actions relating to national quality standards.

Jeanne Ketola, CEO
Pathway Consulting Inc.
Minneapolis, Minnesota
www.pathwayconsultinginc.com

Kathy Roberts, President of Sunrise Consulting Inc., has held various quality engineering and quality management positions in a diverse range of industries during the past 10 years. She has a bachelor's degree in industrial engineering and is an ASQ Certified Quality Auditor and a trained examiner for the North Carolina Performance Excellence Process. Roberts is an active member of the U.S. TAG to TC 176 and is the vice chair of the ANSI Z1 Executive Committee.

Kathy Roberts, President
Sunrise Consulting Inc.
Raleigh, North Carolina
http://thesunrise.home.mindspring.com

Also visit their joint Web site:
www.inanutshellproductions.com

Index

Sections & Clauses

NOTE: Entries in ALL CAPS are clauses from ISO 9001:1994

1994 REQUIREMENTS
4.1 MANAGEMENT RESPONSIBILITY 16–22
4.2 QUALITY SYSTEM 23–26
4.3 CONTRACT REVIEW 5, 27–29, 88
4.4 DESIGN CONTROL 5, 30–33, 98, 100
4.5 DOCUMENT AND DATA CONTROL 34–36
4.6 PURCHASING 37–40
4.7 CONTROL OF CUSTOMER-SUPPLIED PRODUCT 41–42
4.8 PRODUCT IDENTIFICATION AND TRACEABILITY 43–44
4.9 PROCESS CONTROL 45–47, 87
4.10 INSPECTION AND TESTING 48–51
4.11 CONTROL OF INSPECTION, MEASURING, AND TEST EQUIPMENT 52–54
4.12 INSPECTION AND TEST STATUS 43–44, 56–57
4.13 CONTROL OF NONCONFORM-ING PRODUCT 58–60
4.14 CORRECTIVE AND PREVENTIVE ACTION 5, 61–64
4.15 HANDLING, STORAGE, PACK-AGING, PRESERVATION, AND DELIVERY 49, 65–67
4.16 CONTROL OF QUALITY RECORDS 68–71
4.17 INTERNAL QUALITY AUDITS 5, 72–74
4.18 TRAINING 75–77
4.19 SERVICING 47, 49, 78–79
4.20 STATISTICAL TECHNIQUES 80–82

2000 REQUIREMENTS
3 Terms and definitions 38
4 Quality management system 23, 37, 68, 80
4.1 General requirements 17, 23, 24, 80
4.2.1 General 24, 90
4.2.2 Quality manual 24
4.2.3 Control of documents 24, 34, 68, 87
4.2.4 Control of records 68, 87
5 Management responsibility 17, 24, 27, 30, 34, 37, 41, 43, 45, 48, 53, 56, 58, 61, 65, 68, 72, 75, 78, 80
5.1 Management commitment 17
5.2 Customer focus 17, 27, 84, 85
5.3 Quality policy 17, 83
5.4.1 Quality objectives 18
5.4.2 Quality management system planning 18, 24, 26, 84
5.5.1 Responsibility and authority 17
5.5.2 Management representative 18
5.5.3 Internal communication 18, 86
5.6.1 General 17, 18, 70
5.6.2 Review input 18, 58, 61, 63, 72
5.6.3 Review output 19
6 Resource management 19, 25, 27, 31, 34, 35, 38, 41, 43, 45, 49, 53, 56, 58, 61, 65, 69, 72, 75, 78, 80
6.1 Provision of resources 19, 86
6.2.1 General 19, 75
6.2.2 Competence, awareness, and training 19, 69, 70, 75, 91
6.3 Infrastructure 45, 86
6.4 Work environment 45, 87
7 Product realization 19, 25, 27, 35, 38, 41, 43, 49, 53, 56, 59, 62, 66, 69, 73, 76, 78, 81
7.1 Planning of product realization 18, 19, 25, 26, 46, 49, 69
7.2 Customer-related processes 85

7.2.1 Determination of requirements related to the product 28, 85
7.2.2 Review of requirements related to the product 27, 28, 69, 70, 85
7.2.3 Customer communication 28, 62, 85
7.3 Design and development 98
7.3.1 Design and development planning 31
7.3.2 Design and development inputs 31
7.3.3 Design and development outputs 32
7.3.4 Design and development review 31, 32, 69
7.3.5 Design and development verification 31, 69
7.3.6 Design and development validation 32, 69
7.3.7 Control of design and development changes 31, 32, 69
7.4.1 Purchasing process 38, 70
7.4.2 Purchasing information 38
7.4.3 Verification of purchased product 38, 93
7.5.1 Control of production and service provision 46, 49, 53, 66, 78
7.5.2 Validation of processes for production and service provision 46, 70
7.5.3 Identification and traceability 43, 70, 93
7.5.4 Customer property 41–42, 70
7.5.5 Preservation of product 66
7.6 Control of monitoring and measuring devices 53, 70
8 Measurement, analysis, and improvement 20, 25, 28, 32, 35, 39, 42, 44, 46, 49, 54, 57, 59, 62, 66, 70, 73, 76, 78, 81
8.1 General 20, 49, 81
8.2.1 Customer satisfaction 62, 81, 85
8.2.2 Internal audit 70–71, 73, 87
8.2.3 Monitoring and measurement of processes 49, 81
8.2.4 Monitoring and measurement of product 50, 71, 81, 93
8.3 Control of nonconforming product 59, 87
8.4 Analysis of data 81, 83

8.5.1 Continual improvement 20, 62, 73, 82, 83
8.5.2 Corrective action 62, 71, 87
8.5.3 Preventive action 62, 63, 70, 87

A

acceptability
    criteria for 49
acceptable products 41
acceptable subcontractors
    records of 37
access
    documented procedures for 68
accreditation bodies 101
action plan 89
American Society for Quality 1, 102
analysis of data 84
audit checklists 93
audit plan and schedule 93
audit procedure
    scope of 73
audit results 18, 20, 63, 73, 84, 96, 98
auditing 89, 92
auditing issues 97, 101
auditors 93, 94
    internal 89
    third-party 89
audits 93
automotive 98

C

calibration 70
    basis for 70
    process for 52
    records of 70
calibration records 54, 70
calibration status 52
certification bodies 101
cleanliness 87
codes 45
collection
    documented procedures for 68
commitment to quality 16
comparative references 52
competence 76
complaints 28, 62

conforming product 56
consistent pair 99
continual improvement 6,
      23, 82, 83, 95–96
contract amendments 27–28
contract review 27, 29–30, 69–70
   maintaining records of 27, 69
   records of 69–70
contracts 27, 28
control of customer-supplied product 41
control of inspection, measuring, and test
      equipment 52–55
control of nonconforming product 58–60
control of quality records 68–71
control of verification 41
controlled conditions 66
corrective action 18, 62
   on internal audits 72
   records of 62, 71
   results of 71
corrective action activities 62
corrective action implementation 71
   follow-up activities
      records of 71
corrective and preventive action 61–
      64, 84, 96
   procedures for 61
critical product characteristics 30, 32
cross-reference matrix 91
customer 5
customer communication 28, 85
customer complaints 61, 62, 86, 88
   effective handling of 62
customer feedback 28, 62
customer focus 17, 84, 85
customer measures 94
customer needs and expectations 95
customer property 41, 70
   lost, damaged or unsuitable for use
      records of 70
   care of 41
customer requirements 5, 20, 27–
      28, 88, 94
   defining 27, 28
customer satisfaction 19, 81–82, 85–
      86, 88, 95, 97–98
   enhancing 27

customer satisfaction measurement
      system 85
customer satisfaction measures 98
customer service 5
customer-focused organization 6, 95
customer-related processes 85
customer-specific product requirements
      85
customer-supplied product 41–42
customers 58

D

damage and deterioration
      methods to prevent 65
data analysis 20, 96
delivery 65–67
design activity 30
design and development reviews 69
design and/or development input
      requirements 31
Design and/or development outputs 32
design and/or development reviews 32
design and/or development validation 33
design and/or development verification
      33
design control 30–33
design input 30, 32
design output 30, 32
design plans 30
design verification 30
design verification measures 30
design-stage input 33
design-stage input requirements 30
design-stage output 30, 33
designated storage areas 67
   use of 65
disposition of records
   documented procedures for 68
document and data changes 36
document and data control 34–36
document control 36
documentation 23, 89
documentation requirements 87
documented procedures 45, 48, 52
downsizing 84

E

education 75
   records of 69, 75
eight quality management principles 92–94
engineering 5
environmental conditions 52
equipment
   calibration of 52
   records of 45, 47
ergonomics 87
experience 75
   records of 69, 75
external documents 34–35

F

factual approach to decision making 6, 95
feedback from customers 18
filing
   documented procedures for 68
final delivery 66
final inspection 65
final inspection and testing 48
functional management thinking 9, 12
functional perspective
   quiz of 9

G

General documentation requirements 90
goals 16

H

handling 65–67
handling, storage, packaging, preservation, and delivery 65–67
heat 87
humidity 87

I

identification 66
   documented procedures for 68
improvement
   evidence of 98
improvement activities
   facilitation of 82

in-process 50
in-process tests 48
incentives 92
incoming product conformance 48
indexing
   documented procedures for 68
infrastructure 45, 86, 87
inspection activities 50
inspection and test status 56–57
inspection and testing 48–51
inspection and testing activities 48
inspection, measuring, and test equipment 52
   calibration of 54
   calibration records for 70
inspection records 71
internal audit results 72, 94
   records of 72
internal auditing 92
internal auditing requirements 92
internal auditors 93–94, 101
internal audits
   purpose of 73
   results of 70
      records of 70
internal communication 86, 94
internal processing 66
internal quality audits 72–74
involvement of people 6, 95
ISO 10011 2, 92
ISO 10012 1, 54
ISO 10012 Measurement Control System
   1, 99
ISO 10012-1:1992 1
ISO 10012-1:1992 Metrological confir-
   mation system for measuring
   equipment 1
ISO 10012-2:1997 1
ISO 10012-2:1997 Guideline for control
   of measurement processes 1
ISO 14000 98
ISO 14010 101
ISO 14011 101
ISO 14012 101
ISO 19011 2, 92, 99
ISO 19011 Guidelines on quality and/or
   environmental management systems
   auditing 2

ISO 8402 vocabulary 99
ISO 8402:1994 1
ISO 9000 standards family
  modifications to 98
  revisions to 97
ISO 9000-1:1994 1
*ISO 9000:2000 Quality management
  system—Fundamentals and
  vocabulary* 1, 94
ISO 9001:1994 1
*ISO 9001:2000 Quality management
  systems—Requirements* 1
ISO 9002:1994 1
ISO 9003:1994 1
ISO 9004:2000 2
*ISO 9004:2000 Quality management
  systems—Guidelines for perfor-
  mance improvement* 2
ISO Technical Committee 176 2, 6

K

key objectives 95

L

leadership 6, 95

M

maintenance 41, 79
  documented procedures for 68
management 89, 94
management activities 98
management representative 16, 20, 84
management responsibility 16–22
management review
  16–20, 22, 58, 61, 63–64, 70, 72,
  86, 96
  records of 16, 70
management systems 62, 73
manufacturing 102
marking 67
master list 34, 36
measurement capability 52
measurement devices 54
measurement equipment 52
measurement needs

identification of 54
measurement uncertainty 52
measurements 96
monitoring and measurement 49
monitoring and measuring devices 70
mutually beneficial supplier relationships 95

N

noise 87
nonconforming products 58–60
nonconformities
  records of 71

O

objectives 84
obsolete documents
  identification of 35
  inadvertent use of 35
official languages 99
organization 38
organizational objectives 95

P

packaging 65–67
packing 67
Pathway Consulting Inc. 103, 111
performance
  measurements of 85
personnel
  qualifying of 76
  records of 45, 47
plan-do-check-act improvement cycle 26
planning 84
planning activities 84, 94
planning and improvement activities 88
preservation 65–67
preventive action
  procedures for 61
  records for 70
preventive maintenance 87
problem identification 64
problem-solving steps 64
process
  definition of 11
process approach 6, 83, 95

process control 45–47
process goals 95
process management 2, 5–13, 92
process model structure 83
process parameters 45
process performance
    analysis of 18
process perspective
    quiz of 9
process sequence and interaction 24
product
    design and development of 32
product characteristics 45, 50
    monitoring and measurement of 50
product conformance 56
    analysis of 18
product conformity 45, 58
product designs 30
product identification and traceability 43–44
product improvement 19
product in storage
    condition of 65
product nonconformities 61
product realization 6, 46, 89
product release
    authority responsible for 50
product requirements 81, 85
    customer-specific 85
production 5
products
    inspection and test status of 56
    maintenance of 41
proof of capability 52
property of an intellectual nature 42
protection 66
provision of resources 86
purchased product 37
purchasing 37–40
purchasing documents 37–39
    review and approval requirement 38

Q

qualification 76
qualified personnel 45
qualified processes 45, 47, 70
    records of 45, 47, 70

quality assurance 94
quality management system 17–20, 23–
    25, 46, 77, 83–84, 86–87, 89,
    92, 94, 96, 98–100
    performance of 81
quality manual 23–25, 90
quality objectives 16, 18–
    20, 25, 75, 84, 92, 96
quality plan 45–46, 56, 57
quality planning 23, 26, 84
quality planning activities 84
quality policy 16–18, 20–21, 84,
    88, 96
quality procedures 23
quality records 63–64
quality requirements 23
quality system 16, 23–26, 68
quality system documentation 34–35
quality system management 88
quality system requirements 37

R

receiving 50
    methods of 65
receiving inspection 48
record requirements 50
record retention 68
record-keeping requirements 19
record-keeping system 70
    documented procedures for 70
records 34, 93
reference standards 45
registrar 96
Registrar Accreditation Board 102
registration concerns 97
regulatory and statutory requirements 85
repaired and reworked product 58–59
repairs 79
resource management 6
resource needs 19
review and approval requirement 38
review of product requirements 85
revisions
    release of 97
root-cause analysis 64

S

safety 87
sales 5
service 102
    design and development of 32
service and small organizations 97, 102
servicing 78–79
skills 75
special processes 46
    validation of 46
specified requirements 48
statistical techniques 80–82
    documented procedures for 80
stock rooms 67
    use of 65
storage 41, 65–67
    documented procedures for 68
storage areas 65, 67
subcontractor 37–39
subcontractor evaluations
    records of 37, 70
subcontractor records 68, 71
suitable working environment 45
Sunrise Consulting Inc. 103, 111
supplier evaluations 70
    results of 70
supporting services 87
system approach to management 6, 95
systems auditing 94
"systems" perspective 5

T

TAG 2
Task Group 18 2
TC 176 2
technical data 52
telecommunication 98

test hardware 55
test software 52
test software and hardware 54
testing 65
third-party auditors 89, 101
traceability 44, 70
traceable standards 54
training 69–70, 75–77, 89, 91
    documented procedures for 76
    effectiveness of 75
    records of 69–70, 75–76
training, awareness and competency 91
training needs 75–76
training records 69, 75
    types of 77
transition planning 89–96

U

U.S. Standards Group 102
U.S. TAG 3
U.S. Technical Advisory Group 2
unique identification 43, 52
unique identification of products
    records of 70

V

validation 69
validation results 32
verification 69–70
verification and validation activities 49
voice of the customer 84

W

work environment 45, 87
work instructions 23, 45, 66
workmanship criteria 45

Competitive Archaeology in Jordan